Dark Peak
MountainBiking
True Grit Trails

**Vertebrate
Graphics**

Design and production by Vertebrate Graphics Ltd, Sheffield
www.v-graphics.co.uk

Dark Peak
MountainBiking
True Grit Trails

Written by
Paul Evans & **Jon Barton**

Dark Peak
MountainBiking
True Grit Trails

ISBN 0-9548131-0-3

Cover photo: **Andy Heading**

All other Photography by **John Houlihan**
and **Andy Heading**

Design, typesetting and map illustrations by
Vertebrate Graphics Ltd, Sheffield

www.**v-graphics**.co.uk

**Vertebrate
Graphics**

All maps reproduced by permission of Ordnance Survey
on behalf of The Controller of Her Majesty's
Stationery Office. © Crown Copyright. 100025218

Contents

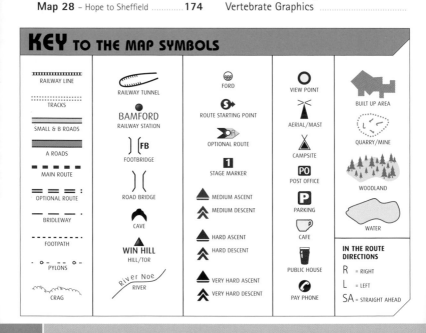

KEY TO THE MAP SYMBOLS

▓▓▓▓▓▓▓ RAILWAY LINE	⌒⌒⌒⌒ RAILWAY TUNNEL	⊖ FORD	◯ VIEW POINT	▓▓ BUILT UP AREA
⋯⋯⋯⋯ TRACKS	● BAMFORD RAILWAY STATION	⬤▶ ROUTE STARTING POINT	⤬ AERIAL/MAST	⟨L⟩ QUARRY/MINE
── SMALL & B ROADS	) (FB FOOTBRIDGE	▶B OPTIONAL ROUTE	⨂ CAMPSITE	🌲 WOODLAND
── A ROADS	) (ROAD BRIDGE	1 STAGE MARKER	PO POST OFFICE	
▬ ▬ ▬ MAIN ROUTE		▲ MEDIUM ASCENT	P PARKING	▬ WATER
═ ═ ═ OPTIONAL ROUTE	⌢ CAVE	⏫ MEDIUM DESCENT	☕ CAFE	
── ── BRIDLEWAY		▲ HARD ASCENT	🍺 PUBLIC HOUSE	**IN THE ROUTE DIRECTIONS**
⋯⋯⋯⋯ FOOTPATH	▲ WIN HILL HILL/TOR	⏫ HARD DESCENT		R = RIGHT
∘ ─ ∘ ─ ∘ PYLONS	River Noe RIVER	▲ VERY HARD ASCENT	☎ PAY PHONE	L = LEFT
⌒⌒⌒ CRAG		⏫ VERY HARD DESCENT		SA = STRAIGHT AHEAD

Introduction

The Dark Peak offers truly world-class riding. The hills of northern Derbyshire are crisscrossed with ancient roads and flowing moorland singletrack. Fabulous descents come in all varieties – fast, loose, rocky, rutted and rooty – and The Peak has a fierce collection of climbs: uphill slogs, loose uphill slogs, technical, loose and rocky uphill slogs – most, thankfully, within easy reach of refuelling at local cafés and pubs.

The Dark Peak is real mountain biking: hard on your body, hard on components and offers plenty of experiences that will leave you eager to return again and again. Personally we can't get enough of those fabulous 'rock gardens', the descent from Rushop Edge being a prime example, where a dry stream bed drops down forming a series of rocky steps: flowing, perfectly formed drop-offs that max out suspension and max out the grin-factor.

In this book we supply you with 'the beta' that will take you right to the brink of our world-class downhills, carry you joyously across silver-grey ribbons of moorland track and then challenge you mightily with some real beasts of climbs.

All this action takes place in an area of outstanding natural beauty, with breathtaking views and the opportunity to glimpse some very interesting wildlife – not least an increasing number of other mountain bikers, avidly keen to enjoy the delights of the Dark Peak.

Needless to say, a beautiful place like this demands respect. Please stick to rights of way and please present a friendly, courteous face to the other folks enjoying yet another superb day out in the Dark Peak.

We aim to please, so if you find anything wrong with this guide, why not contact us at: **www.v-graphics.co.uk**

Paul Evans & Jon Barton

Acknowledgments

The Authors would like to thank the following people for support and assistance: Brian Gibb at Endura, Jonathan Bell at Gore, Cullen Ward at ATB Sales/Marin, Caroline Griffiths and Tim Davies at Madison, Simon Gershon and all the team at Gearshift/Orbit Cycles, Steve Young at Lumicycle, Mark at Singletrack, Nicky Birkin, Robin Barker, Ingrid Crossland at First Ascent, Grálnne Coakley, Paul Hopkins at the Peak Park, Jane Robinson and Richard Wheeldon at Cordee, Alan James at Rockfax, Simon Swallow, Richard Manterfield, Bethany Marshall, Stephen Lovell, Caroline Essery and David Evans, Shaun Leatherbarrow, Kevin Manterfield and Dave Black.

Rights of Way

To the best of our knowledge, all of the routes in this guide are totally legal, in other words, mountain bikers have what is termed 'Right of Way'. The following information is provided to help ensure that your ride is legal should you need to adapt your route (shorten or extend your ride) or if you're planning a route of your own from your OS map.

All outdoor folk, including mountain bikers, have to stick to rights of way. Unlike Sweden or Germany, for example, we're not allowed just to wander around the great outdoors willy-nilly, just as we please.

There are a lot of good reasons for sticking to rights of way – here are just a few:

1. We've not always had the right of access to The Peak that we enjoy today. Some pioneering folk have had to work very hard to gain this access from the landowners and it would be a very bad thing to risk jeopardising this hard-won freedom through careless or ill-informed actions.
2. Technically speaking, you're committing trespass if you ride on a footpath – no matter how wide – and you could be prosecuted by a landowner for any damage caused. Also, most sensible people would rather avoid the embarrassment involved in this kind of encounter or confrontation.
3. Riding on footpaths upsets walkers. Again, not worth the aggro – and they've every right to enjoy their day.
4. Sticking to rights of way helps preserve fragile moorland habitats.
5. Riding through overgrown greenery plays havoc with your cassette and jockey wheels.

Rights of Way Include:

Bridleways

Trails for horses, dudes! Mountain bikers have the right to share bridleways with walkers and horses – but take care, horses spook easily (*see page 60 – Trail Tip 4*).

Byways Open to All Traffic

Otherwise known as BOATs, these allow all traffic to pass, including vehicles – although, surprisingly, I've yet to see a boat on a BOAT. This means that you may well be sharing the trail with motorcyclists and 4WD enthusiasts – often to be seen enjoying the peace, quiet and fresh air of the countryside.

Forest Tracks and Paths

Officially, you need permission to ride through Forestry Commission land. Often however (as is the case with areas of Wharncliffe Woods) this permission has already been granted, and the Forestry Commission generally regards cycling favourably. A note of caution – beware of forestry operations, because a fully loaded logging truck could easily dent your bike!

Green Lanes

A non-legal term for an unsurfaced country road. There is some debate at the moment as to who's allowed to use them, but mountain bikers have nothing to worry about at present.

White Roads

Most roads on OS maps have colours that indicate their status, white roads have no colour and so have no recorded right of way status. When looking at the map, these often appear to be farm tracks or private roads when, in fact, they are public highways. Of the estimated 7000km of 'lost' white roads around the UK, many are great, totally legal trails. Unfortunately, you need to check with the definitive map at your local highway authority to be absolutely sure. If in doubt stick to a bridleway marked on your OS map. **NB.** If you're not already familiar with the symbols on your OS map denoting bridleways, footpaths and so on, check out the *Public Rights of Way* in the *Customer Information* section on your map.

Signs

Not all footpaths and bridleways are signed. To make matters more confusing, rights of way can change in status (in other words, some bridleways get 'downgraded' to footpaths and some footpaths get 'upgraded' to bridleways) without the signs being changed. What this means is that there is not necessarily any clear indication 'on the ground' as to whether that wide trail that you want to follow is an illegal footpath or a legal bridleway. That's why it's a good idea to carry an OS map with you on every ride.

Some paths have coloured way-marking arrows, these mean:

Yellow: Footpaths (you're not allowed to ride on footpaths, remember)
Blue: Bridleways
Red: Byways that can be used by everyone

Some forestry areas, such as Wharncliffe Woods, also have way-marked cycle routes. These colouring systems usually indicate the difficulty of the route – look out for explanatory notices at the roadhead.

Rules of the Off Road

Only hooligans enjoy the stress of conflict. The mountain biking community deserves a big pat on the back for keeping it chill on the hill – let's help keep it that way:

1. Always Ride Legal (see note on rights of way)
2. Ride with consideration for others
3. Give way to horses and pedestrians – avoid natural habitats, animals and crops
4. Close all gates
5. Take your litter home
6. Help keep water sources clean – don't take toilet stops near streams
7. Avoid the risk of fire
8. Keep the noise down
9. Be self sufficient for you and your bike
10. Enjoy the countryside and respect its life and work

Safety

This book is aimed at the fit and technically accomplished mountain biker. All of the routes described are challenging and may include very tough climbs and steep (some potentially dangerous) descents. A complete circuit of any of these routes without a 'foot-down', especially on-sight, will deserve a pat on the back – or even a pint!

Warning

Some of these routes venture into mountainous terrain. If you are planning to tackle any of these (the Kinder Circuit is a good example) you'll need a bit of what's best described as mountain 'savvy'– particularly on shorter, winter days.

Set out properly equipped and properly clothed, carry plenty of water and ensure that you're properly hydrated. Take your spares, a pump and some food. Even if it's warm in the valley, you'll welcome the extra comfort of a windproof if you're taking a snack stop higher up – and this could help avert the dangers of hypothermia in the event of an accident. Pack a good light-source if there's a risk of finishing in the dark.

The ability to read a map and navigate in poor visibility should also be treated as essential. Riding in a group is safer and usually more fun – make sure that you don't leave the slower members of your party too far behind.

Always allow more time than you think is necessary. Bear in mind that a day out with a big group (say five or more in the party) will incur time penalties, as you'll almost inevitably be dealing with 'mechanicals'.

If you are planning to ride alone, take careful stock of the potential seriousness of an accident – you could be without assistance for a considerable length of time. Always tell someone where you are going and when you plan to get back. If you have a mobile phone then take it with you – but be aware that reception in The Peak is patchy.

As the area is justifiably popular with other users (and to minimise demands on the National Health Service) we strongly recommend an aptitude versus attitude approach – in other words, please ride within your ability.

On hot, sunny days, make sure that you slap on that Factor 30+ and **always wear your helmet.**

Mountain Rescue
In the event of an accident requiring mountain rescue assistance:
Dial 999 and ask for **POLICE – MOUNTAIN RESCUE**

How to Use This Book

This book should provide you with all of the information that you need for an enjoyable, trouble free and successful ride. The following tips should also be of help:

1. We strongly recommend that you invest in these two maps: *Ordnance Survey Explorer*® OI 1 1:25,000 The Peak District, Dark Peak Area and *Ordnance Survey Explorer*® OL24 (1:25,000) The Peak District White Peak Area. These are essential even if you are familiar with the area – you may need to cut the ride short or take an alternative route.

2. Choose your route. Consider the time you have available and the abilities/level of experience of all members your party – then read the safety section of this guide.

3. We recommend that you study the route description carefully before setting off. Cross-reference this to your OS map so that you've got a good sense of general orientation in case you need an escape route. Make sure that you are familiar with the symbols used on the maps.

4. Get out there and get dirty.

Grading of Routes

You'll notice that we have graded the routes (and certain key climbs/descents within them) on the basis of the Green, Blue, Red and Black system that appears to be increasingly accepted at mountain bike centres around the UK.

This is roughly similar to the system used in skiing where ▲ = Easy, ▲ = Medium, ▲ = Hard and ▲ = Extreme.

Note. Where a route doesn't fit easily into the grading system above, we've used the following symbol to indicate intermediate levels of grading: **》** (e.g. ▲**》**▲ indicates a hard red or an easy black!)

The routes are graded for average summer conditions. In a drought they might feel easier, in the depths of winter after three weeks of freeze/thaw action they might feel a little bit trickier. Consideration has been given to such issues as technical severity, length and remoteness. The grades are subjective, the kind of time you have on a given route, or even a specific downhill or climb, will be dictated by your personal levels of fitness, skill and bottle. We hope that we've achieved a balance in our grading that will

meet with the approval of the average, non-specialist rider. At least there should be some value in this for pub debates.

Note: Maps, Descriptions, Distances
While every effort has been made to maintain accuracy within the maps and descriptions in this guide, we have had to process a vast amount of information and we are unable to guarantee that every single detail is correct.

Please exercise caution if a direction appears at odds with the route on the map. If in doubt, a comparison between the route, the description and a quick cross-reference to your OS map (along with a bit of common sense) should help ensure that you're on the right track. Note that distances have been measured off the map – these may not tally with your bike computer as map distances rarely coincide 100% with distances on the ground (and you may have to carry your bike at times).

Please treat stated distances as a guideline only.

Bike Set Up

Tyres
The Peak's many rocky descents cry out for tyres of a width of 2"+ with square edge knobbles, run at a sensible pressure to avoid snake-bites. You'll be especially grateful for the extra cushioning if you're riding a hard tail.

Frame and Forks
A full suspension frame is not essential, but it will be found to be a great ally on technical ground and will certainly ease the impact of a long day in the saddle on one of our enduro circuits. We've been riding the *Marin Rift Zone* and *Rock Springs* over the last couple of seasons – both excellent bikes.

Brakes
Disc brakes, in addition to their superb stopping power, offer great reliability in muddy conditions and we're treating them as pretty well essential – especially in the winter. Pads may wear out alarmingly quickly in the gritty conditions so choose a hard-wearing compound or bring spares.

Kit

Maps
Ordnance Survey Explorer® OL1 (1:25,000) The Peak District Dark Peak Area
Ordnance Survey Explorer® OL24 (1:25,000) The Peak District White Peak Area

Hydration Pack
Way better then lugging around water bottles. We've been using *Platypus* hydration packs to avoid getting thirsty.

Clothing
The tried and tested layering system utilising 'technical' fabrics (**not cotton**) in a base layer/fleece/wind- or waterproof shell combination works great, especially in winter. As mountain biking is a very active sport, it's worth setting off just a little on the cool side- this should keep you comfortable on the first section, which is usually uphill. Don't, however, make the mistake of leaving those essential warm layers behind. You'll need them on the descents and during snack breaks. There are a few good companies, for example *Endura* and *Gore*, that manufacture quality cycle clothing that can be relied upon in British conditions.

Gloves
Essential – especially in the event of a spill. Make sure that you've got the gloves to fit the season (winter gloves are uncomfortably sweaty in the summer, summer gloves mean numb fingers and a lack of braking response in the winter).

Other Essentials
Don't leave home without a good pump that you're familiar with, spare inner tubes, puncture repair kit and multi-tool. You will need some trail food too.

Thanks to:

Night Riding

Night riding opens up a whole new world of mountain biking enjoyment. Now it is possible to enjoy a mid-week ride of up to two hours (more if you're carrying extra battery juice) in your favourite off-road playground. Night riding is brilliant fun, but it's a completely different ball game out there on a winter's night and (hardly surprisingly) there are a few risks to be aware of. To help stay out of trouble, here are a few tips:

Lights and Batteries

Invest in the best lighting system that you can afford (we've been using the very excellent *Lumicycle* lights over the winter). A helmet mount is superior to a bar mounting on technical ground. Ensure that your battery is fully charged up before you ride. Carry a secondary light source such as a head torch for emergencies. Ensure that you pack a rear light for road sections and keep it clean of mud.

Route Planning and Safety

Choose your ride on the basis of the manufacturer's minimum battery life and allow extra time – you will be slower in the dark. Stay on ground that you are familiar with at first (night-time navigation in unfamiliar territory demands military expertise) and not too far from major roads. Always ride with a friend. Make sure that someone knows where you're going and when to expect you back.

Ride within your limits – trees loom up very quickly in the dark!

PHOTO COURTESY OF LUMICYCLE

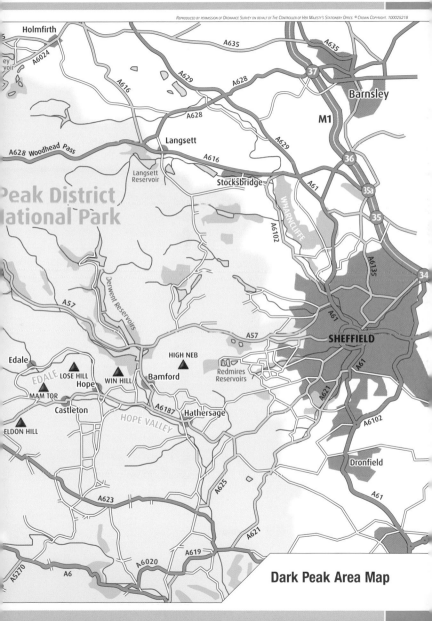

Dark Peak Area Map

Classics

sponsored by

SECTION 1

Classics

Classics

Weighing in low on the kilometres, these short rides are ideal for the time starved mountain biker. Whilst you'll never be very far from civilisation on a Classic (they make excellent night rides or are ideal for a quick after work blast), they are packed with interest and often venture quickly into wild terrain – make sure you pack a waterproof.

'OPTION A' ON THE BLACKA MOOR CIRCUIT **PHOTO:** *ANDY HEADING*

Blacka Moor – East Peak

Introduction

An excursion onto the moors west of Sheffield. This is a glorious, tight little circuit that maximises the quality singletrack potential of this area – and it can be savoured in around an hour.

The Ride

A short road section leads quickly to a five bar gate and then it's out across the moorland on an exposed and (usually) boggy jeep track. This becomes increasingly technical until a steep descent takes us down at some speed to a secretive junction with the unique singletrack skirting left round the base of Wimble Holme Hill. A fast descent with an exhilarating stream crossing follows. You then have the option of **A**: a very challenging climb; or **B**: some gruelling road work, either of which will take you round onto Houndkirk Road – a superb section of 'desert high road' that wouldn't be out of place in Utah! From here it's a swift cruise downhill back to the car park.

BLACKA MOOR   GRADE: ▲

DISTANCE: 12.5KM (OPTION B)   **TOTAL ASCENT:** 358M
START/FINISH: LONGSHAW NATIONAL TRUST ESTATE
GRID REFERENCE: 267 800   **PARKING:** LONGSHAW NATIONAL TRUST ESTATE CAR PARK
CAFÉ: LONGSHAW VISITORS CENTRE Tel: 01433 631 708
PUBLIC HOUSE: THE FOX HOUSE Tel: 01433 630 374

IN THE WOODS ON THE BLACKA MOOR CIRCUIT **PHOTO:** *ANDY HEADING*

PHOTO: *ANDY HEADING*

N

0 miles

0 km

BUR
MO

Parson House
(Outdoor Pursuit Centre)

HATHERSAGE

Fox House
Inn

A6187

B6521

Longshaw
Country
Park

B6055

Totley

CALVER

MAP 02

1

E

RINGINGLOW

Sheephill Road

Houndkirk Road

3

A625

Dore Moor

SHEFFIELD ▶

A625

Whitelow Farm

New Whitelow Farm

Whitelow Road

Blacka Moor

Blacka Plantation

Dore

2

Totley Moor

Wimble Holme Hill

ir Shaft

SHEFFIELD ▶

OWLER BAR

A621

Totley

Blacka Moor

Directions – Blacka Moor

1 R out of **Longshaw NT Estate car park** onto road (B6055) **»** Easily uphill on tarmac to junction with B6405 (coming from L) and five bar gate **»** SA through gate on wide sandy track passing air shaft on L after 1km **»** Just past air shaft cross junction with track coming from L, don't join this track but bear slightly R (boggy, heavily rutted) following least boggy ground (best on L) but keeping in touch with jeep track on R to join narrowing track **»** Follow track, which bears L and begins to descend with increasing interest **»** Approx. 50m **before first gate**, very indistinct bridleway bears down and L (just on crest of last drop before gate), crossing small hollow then up to join very narrow singletrack skirting base of Wimble Holme Hill (steep drop on R!) **»** Descend slightly, RW through gate, cross field to gate on R by clump of trees

2 SA, exciting descent to junction with path coming up from R **»** SA through gap in wall between gateposts **»** down into trees, excellent twisting descent eventually dropping through ford to junction with wider path **»** Two options available here: Turn L for very challenging climb SA up through trees to road (A625) **»** Turn R down A625, take first L (Sheephill Road) or:

OptionalRoute

Turn R, follow path to track and then join tarmac **»** L up Whitelow Road – fairly steep road work – to join A625 **»** R down A625, take first L (Sheephill Road)

3 Continue along Sheephill Road, slightly uphill, cross stream, look out for bridleway on L **»** L through gate to join bridleway, up fairly steep, stony path for 0.5km to four way junction with sandy track **»** L here, good riding for 2.75km – track eventually descends quickly to gate

4 SA through gate to join A625 **»** Turn R, downhill to Fox House Inn **»** Turn L, descend slightly to **Longshaw NT Estate car park** on R

JON BARTON ON CLASSIC WOODLAND SINGLETRACK **PHOTO:** ANDY HEADING

BIG SKY ABOVE NEW MILLS **PHOTO:** JOHN HOULIHAN

Chinley Churn – West Peak

Introduction

This hilly outpost of the Peak District National Park, somewhat overshadowed by its grander neighbours and neglected by all but a few sheep and a pair of ravens, is actually one of the country's best kept mountain biking secrets (or at least it was until now!). Crisscrossed by singletrack, all manner of all-weather, all-terrain cycling exists – from great value training and get fit mini loops, to challenging ascents and fast downhills.

The Ride

Our circuit takes in the best of Chinley Churn, starting from the convenient base of **New Mills**. Climbing up and over the summit, a short, fast descent leads to a brilliant section of adventurous single-track, and a tough ascent, along the eastern and northern flanks of the hill. Enjoy the fast track descent to the valley, because it's almost immediately back up onto the hill before a delightful, varied descent leads back towards the Sett Valley Trail and New Mills.

CHINLEY CHURN   GRADE: ▲»▲

DISTANCE: 15KM   **TOTAL ASCENT:** 564M
START/FINISH: NEW MILLS MARKET STREET CAR PARK
GRID REFERENCE: 000 857   **PARKING:** THERE IS AMPLE PARKING IN NEW MILLS,
CAFÉ: BRING SANDWICHES!   AND LIMITED PARKING ON LANESIDE ROAD
PUBLIC HOUSE: THE WALTZING WEASEL Tel: 01663 743 402
          (One of the best bar meals in the UK & accommodation. www.w-weasel.co.uk)

High Lee

New Mills

Sett Valley

Hidebank

S

8

2 Lo
Leigh

Lane

A6015

← STOCKPORT

Newtown

A6(1)

Gow

Furness Vale

Buxton →

MAP 03

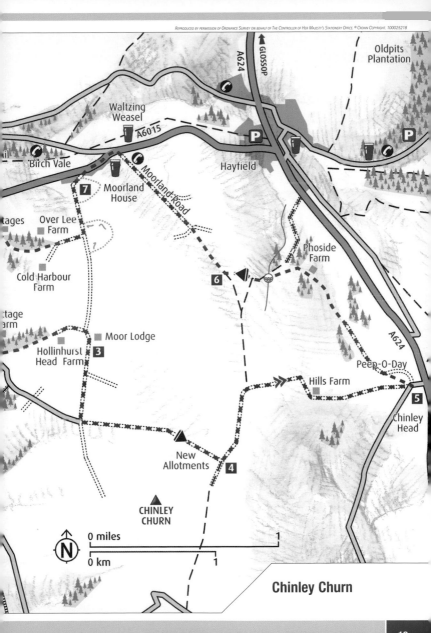

Oldpits
Plantation

GLOSSOP

A624

Waltzing
Weasel

A6015

Hayfield

P

P

Birch Vale

Moorland House

Moorland Road

7

Over Lee
Farm

Phoside
Farm

Cold Harbour
Farm

6

ttages
arm

Moor Lodge

A624

Hollinhurst
Head Farm

3

Peep-O-Day

Hills Farm

5

Chinley
Head

New
Allotments

4

CHINLEY
CHURN

N

0 miles   1

0 km   1

Chinley Churn

Directions – Chinley Churn

1 From **Market Street car park**, R out of car park onto Market Street **»** R along Market Street to mini-roundabout **»** L down hill towards traffic lights on Union Road - junction of Bridge Street (B6101) and Church Road (A6015), direction Hayfield **»** Turn L, cross bridge, follow A6015 towards Hayfield for about 900m **»** Turn R into Laneside Road, on curve in road next to tool hire shop

2 Climb up Laneside Road (alternative start point) for approx. 700m, look out for track marked *Bridleway* on L **»** Turn L, SA past cottage on L **»** SA through gate climb easily up grassy track through fields, stream on L **»** Go through gate into Hollinhurst Head Farm, continue SA up to meet main track at Moor Lodge

3 Turn R along track for 800m, pass farm on L **»** Turn L at four-way junction – follow track marked *Bridleway* up through gate into the hills! First section is stony, walled track resembling a stream bed **»** Through next gate the ascent gets easier before next gate **»** SA through gate, take a rest. The next climb, to New Allotments, of approx. 500m is a serious challenge, but not impossible!

4 Turn L and follow rutted singletrack N **»** After 500m, through a new gate, take bridle-way straight on across moor (ignore bridleway descending to L) **»** Keeping close to fence and wall on R, follow track, eventually passing through gate to descend through Hills Farm (please walk your bike through the garden) **»** Descend farm road 1km to just before gate and junction with metalled road coming from R (near main road) at Peep-o-Day

5 Go through gate on L (signposted *To Birch Vale and Hayfield via Phoside and Ridge Top*) **»** Follow indistinct path across field, aiming initially for finger post then gate in bottom corner of field **»** Better singletrack soon contours around hill **»** Go past Phoside Farm on R, heading L uphill to gate by woodland **»** Through gate, cross stream and then climb (push!) up hill following the valley **»** Take R fork at fingerpost, for fine, rideable singletrack ascent to alight on broad moorland ridge (this climb is a great descent – give it a go, it isn't too far to come back up again!)

6 Turn R down hill and pass through gate – three very fast kilometres down Moorland Road to arrive in Birch Vale **»** Turn L on the main road, after 200m turn L up steep hill on quarry road

7 Pass quarry on L, turn R down farm track after 400m (signed *Cold Harbour Farm*) **»** Descend good farm track straight on **»** Ignore track to L (private), go slowly and with respect through Over Lee Farm (route is SA through their large gate, then across garden and through small gate on other side) **»** Descend by stream through delightful mixed hobbit habitat, bear L at junction at next cluster of buildings, past dilapidated barn to L, where track curves R and descends to main road

8 Turn L, look out for bridleway joining road at acute angle from R **»** Turn R onto bridleway, follow this across field and skirt housing estate on L **»** Cross road, through gate (signposted *Public Bridleway*), turn L along Sett Valley Trail to its end of cycle access • Turn R turn on to the road, follow road RW across bridge **»** Turn L, climb steeply back up to **New Mills Market Street**

CLIMBING CHINLEY CHURN **PHOTO:** JOHN HOULIHAN

FAST AND LOOSE ON THE DIGLEY CIRCUIT **PHOTO:** *JOHN HOULIHAN*

Digley Circuit – North Peak

Introduction

Short, fast, fun and almost entirely lacking in level ground. A good intro to mountain biking, or as a training circuit – excellent whatever the weather or season. Highly recommended as a night ride.

The Ride

The route gets better and better the further you navigate round, which is good news as the start is straight into a long tarmac hill-climb, before dropping down Harden Hill into... the middle of nowhere. Back on the tarmac for a long climb, the going gets increasing rough, joining a superb moorland singletrack before crossing the Holmfirth to Mossley Road (A635). The fantastic long, descending track back to the car park is a fitting finale.

DIGLEY CIRCUIT   GRADE: ▲

DISTANCE: 11.5KM

START/FINISH: DIGLEY RESERVOIR

PARKING: CAR PARK ON S SIDE OF THE DAM

PUBLIC HOUSE: FORD INN Tel: 01484 854 741

TOTAL ASCENT: 392M

GRID REFERENCE: 109 068

CAFÉ: BRING SANDWICHES!

PHOTO: *ANDY HEADING*

PHOTO: *JOHN HOULIHAN*

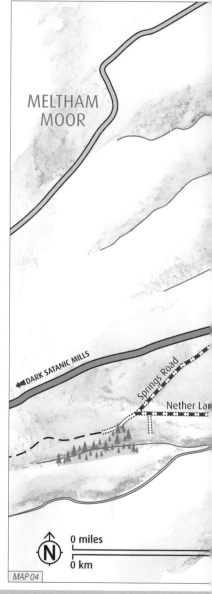

MELTHAM
MOOR

◄ DARK SATANIC MILLS

Springs Road

Nether La

0 miles

0 km

N

MAP 04

B6107

Royd Bridge

2

Upper Royd

Royd Farm

Ash Royd

Magdalen Road

Harden Hill Road

Snape Reservoir

ROUND HILL

Ford Inn

HOLMFIRTH ▶

Green Gate Road

The Huntsman

A635

3

Acres Lane

P

Bilberry Reservoir

Digley Reservoir

P

S

Long Walls

HOLMFIRTH ▶

Holmbridge

WOODHEAD ◀

A6024

1

Digley Circuit

Directions – Digley Circuit

1 L out of **Digley Reservoir southern car park** and across dam **»** L at T-junction, then up road climb for 1.3km keeping to Green Gate Road, there are occasional blue pictures of cycles to encourage you **»** L at crossroads with main road at Ford Inn **»** Follow main road (A635) for 400m to a R turn onto a track signed bridleway **»** Follow this right of way, past mounds of earth to join a long rutted and loose descent to Royd Bridge

2 L along road and uphill **»** Follow this road, ignoring bridleway which leads SA **»** Follow road, turning R at bridleway signed *Ash Royd Farm* **»** Passing farms on the L and R, continue SA as road turns to track then through a gate onto a superb moorland singletrack, ascending Round Hill **»** Called Magdalen Road, this singletrack, often faint (keep the wall to your L to help navigate) is pretty well rideable in dry conditions, if a little technical in places **»** Eventually the gate at the summit is reached **»** A short descent past another gate reaches the A635

3 Turn R then almost immediately L down the track of Springs Road (Signposted *Bridleway*) **» Beware a very large boulder in the middle of the track**, especially you fast night-riders **»** Follow this paved track to a sharp turn L just before a gate and stile **»** Follow track to the L, superb fast descent along Nether Lane, for 2.5km with a short rise soon reaching a gate then a road **»** R on the road to a crossroads **»** Turn R downhill, cross the dam and R into **Digley Reservoir southern car park**

Langsett – North Peak

Introduction

Exceptionally useful espresso-type ride, offering concentrated enjoyment in a small but beautifully formed package. Ideal for the time-starved mountain biker, this is a great quality, super-varied moorland experience that can be enjoyed in just over an hour.

The Ride

Easy road-work leads to a gentle rolling warm up through woods. From here the route joins a quality singletrack ascent that gets really wild very quickly, maintaining interest all the way before joining the Cut Gate Path emerging from the heart of the Dark Peak. A great quality descent then brings you down into the woods and across the busy A616 for a short but worthwhile detour into farmland. Then it's back to the car park.

LANGSETT   GRADE: ▲

DISTANCE: 10KM
START/FINISH: LANGSETT
PARKING: LANGSETT BARN CAR PARK
PUBLIC HOUSE: WAGON AND HORSES, LANGSETT Tel: 01266 763 147

TOTAL ASCENT: 297M
GRID REFERENCE: 211 004
CAFÉ: BANK VIEW CAFÉ Tel: 01226 762 337

trail tips

1 Look B4 U leap

If you're used to the manufactured trails of Coed-y-Brenin, South Wales Forestry Centres and Dalby Forest, you'll be used to riding tracks that have been manufactured with chain-ring clearances in mind! The trails in The Peak are all-natural, so if in doubt get off your bike, check that drop-off and avoid that painful 'endo'

PHOTO: ANDY HEADING

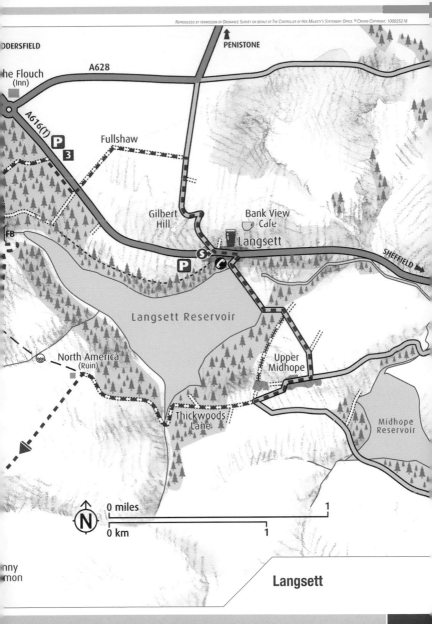

ODDERSFIELD

PENISTONE

he Flouch
(Inn)

A628

A616(T)

P 3

Fullshaw

FB

Gilbert
Hill

Bank View
Cafe

Langsett

S

P

SHEFFIELD

Langsett Reservoir

North America
(Ruin)

Upper
Midhope

Thickwoods
Lane

Midhope
Reservoir

0 miles   1

N

0 km   1

nny
mon

Langsett

Directions – Langsett

1 R out of **Langsett Barn car park** onto busy A616 » Down hill through Langsett – look out for R turn just after Wagon and Horses pub – Midhope Cliff Lane (minor road) » Turn R, cross dam then follow road round to R through hamlet of Upper Midhope » Approx. 250m past hamlet, road takes sharp L turn at which metalled track of Thickwoods Lane (unsigned) heads SA » Follow track through woodland, through two gates then up and along side of woods to ruins of North America Farm – **do not go through gate into ruins** » Turn L (wall on R) to join great singletrack ascent » Continue SA across moor for 1.5km to join Cut Gate Path coming from L

2 R along Mickledon Edge (Cut Gate), follow loose, stony path, mainly in descent, but with one short sharp climb » Quality descent, with good jumps, continues, dropping into steeper, rocky section before track smoothes out and drops down to foot bridge – get into low gear before gate » Through gate, cross bridge to short sharp climb up stony track » At top of climb follow main track, head SA on smooth forestry track, following it round R to edge of A616

3 R along concessionary bridleway that runs parallel to A616 until end after 200m » Cross A616 to join bridleway on opposite side » Up wide farm track (often muddy) between two stone walls before dropping down » Turn R onto Gilbert Hill (minor road) » Down Gilbert Hill to join A616 » Turn R for a few metres, turn L into **Langsett Barn car park**

Rowarth Circuit – West Peak

Introduction

Tucked away in a quiet corner of the National Park, this ride takes in some lovely varied terrain and commands magnificent views over to the **High Peak**, **Kinder** and **Chinley Churn** routes.

The ride is described for optimum dry weather conditions – giving the experienced rider every chance of styling the whole circuit. In anything but drought conditions, the route in reverse is probably better, as the boggy ground is all on the descent.

The Ride

The route warms up along country lanes before cutting across Coombes Tor, dropping down to the base of Lantern Pike, then up over the hill, and around its southern flank to follow an excellent track and rocky descent back into Rowarth. Its main features are singletrack, rocky descents and a very good chance of solitude.

ROWARTH CIRCUIT   GRADE: ▲»▲

DISTANCE: 13KM
START/FINISH: ROWARTH
PARKING: OPPOSITE THE LITTLE MILL INN
PUBLIC HOUSE: LITTLE MILL INN, ROWARTH Tel: 01663 743 178

TOTAL ASCENT: 382M
GRID REFERENCE: 012 889
CAFÉ: BRING A LUNCH BOX!

PHOTO: ANDY HEADING

Quarry
(disused)

Ludworth
Moor

0 miles

0 km

MAP 06

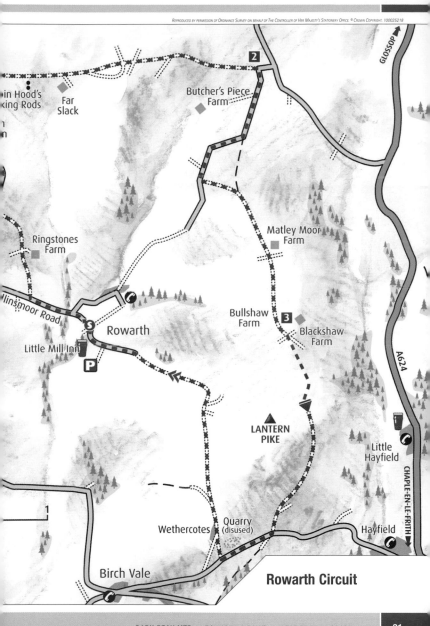

Rowarth Circuit

Directions – Rowarth Circuit

1   L out of car park past pub onto Hollinsmoor Rd **»** Climb gently up tarmac, ignoring R turn to *Rowarth Only* **»** Take next R turn onto farm track to Ringstones Farm **»** SA past farm on rough double track **»** Turn R at road, past Pistol Farm on L and Gun Farm on R **»** Turn R at bridleway (signed) almost on brow of hill **»** Follow track, taking R fork after 150m **»** Through gate, follow track, through second gate and pass Robins Hoods Picking Rods (you'll know them when you see them) **»** Continue past farm buildings on R, through gate, singletrack bridleway climbs up hill with wall on R and fence on L – technical and boggy in parts! **»** Track turns L, then R through gate and over col **»** Make rocky descent onto farm track, descend SA to gate

2   Just past gate turn R on tarmac road **»** Follow this road mainly in descent for approx. one km, turn L uphill onto hardpack signed *Bridleway* erroneously shown as a path on OS map (straight on is road then bridleway, back into Rowarth) **»** Follow path, then good track through a couple of gates along to Matleymoor Farm on L **»** SA past farm, follow track mainly in descent to L turn in track at base of hill

3   R through gate **»** There are six choices here! Follow bridleway (signed *Hayfield via Lantern Pike*) – this track is indistinct across a rough field, aim for the small gate and little bit of track just visible over to your L (with your back to the gate, this is at roughly 10 o'clock) **»** Across field and through gate, stiff, loose climb up and over hill **»** Fast, loose descent leads down to road – pay heed to the warning signs that tell of impending doom for those with failing breaks! **»** Turn R at bottom onto tarmac road, climb up steeply for 400m to brow of hill **»** Turn R past quarry onto farm track **»** Pass farm with lots of barking dogs on L **»** SA at junction with old track on L **»** Take L fork as track starts to descend **»** Follow excellent rocky track, mainly in descent, to junction with tarmac road, just past steep section **»** Continue SA past farm on L and house on R (signed *Long Lee Private Road*) to car park

TOP TEN SINGLETRACK
IN THE DARK PEAK

Dark Peak singletrack has its own, unique character – short, sharp, offering concentrated technical value. Littered with ruts, bomb holes and rocky sections – often in glorious high moorland settings – this selection is guaranteed to leave a lasting impression on the mind of any serious mountain biker.

1   **Howden Edge to Slippery Stones (Cut Gate)** The section of descent from the 'col' at Howden Edge is a singletrack classic. Beginning steep and rutted, a thin strip of dirt then breaks out across the open moor. Things soon become narrow, stony and loose past a couple of hairpins to the rock steps. Don't miss the signposted left turn on this last section – you will be approaching it fast and there's still a great little hairpin to come. Very satisfying!

2   **Derwent Edge** In dry conditions this becomes a text-book ribbon of silvery-grey, gritty sand. Quite wide now, and unfortunately getting wider, 'ethical riding' makes this a real blast in descent.

3   **Cut Gate to North America** Not overly long, but very scenic, this great little portion of moorland can be as tricky as you want to make it (take care with your line choices!). A superb variety of surfaces and some great opportunities to grab air make this lovely section of singletrack a real winner.

4   **Wharncliffe** At its best in the drier months, Wharncliffe is littered with quality singletrack. The second of the singletrack sections described in our Wharncliffe Cross Country Circuit is a superb, technical blast, littered with a smorgasbord of rock gardens, bombholes and roots.
Honorary North York's Moors.

5   **The Knott** A really peachy section of rolling, moorland trail. The only real interruption to this fast and flowing feast is the ford about a third of the way along – but even this should be style-able with a bit of luck and cunning use of gears.

6   **Win Hill** O.K. it's mostly a climb, but the much photographed singletrack section up the southern flanks of Win Hill is an essential rite-of passage for any mountain biker – and the views just keep getting better and better.

7   **Chinley Churn** This oddly-named and seldom visited western outpost of the Dark Peak is criss-crossed by loads of great quality singletrack - all full of character. Best in the dry, this is a great little hill to explore at leisure.

8   **Wharncliffe Singletrack Special** A very sweet section of singletrack through trees - tight, twisty, littered with user friendly obstacles - and great in the dry. Co-ordinates available for download from our website.

9   **Wimble Holme Hill** A very short section of singletrack that's included here because it comes with an almost unique penalty for failure - on the right hand side is a steep rocky drop down into the bilberrys. Actually quite a test of nerve and balance to style, it's livened up by a couple of black squelchy bog holes – obviously designed by nature's great trailbuilder to catch out the unwary!

10 **Robin Hoods Picking Rods** Another short - but great quality - section of technical riding across moorland that is quite remote in feeling. Pretty much a climb, the gradient is still friendly enough to make the humps, ruts and other obstacles ride-able – drier conditions offer a better chance of success.

Epics

sponsored by

www.endura.co.uk

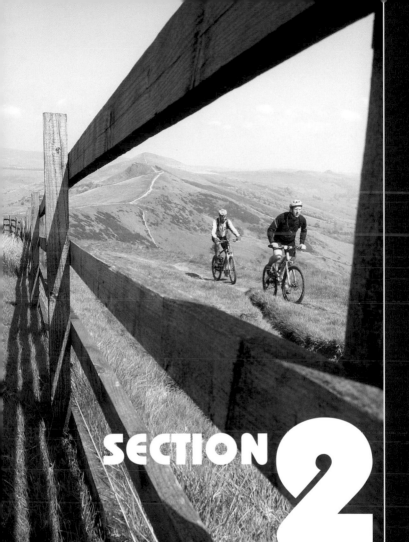

SECTION 2

Epics

PHOTO: *ANDY HEADING*

Epics

Full day experiences, offering enjoyable riding coupled with proper challenges – either a good helping of distance, gruelling uphills or some serious downhill action ...whichever of these epic rides you choose from, you're in for some solid riding.

ENJOYING THE SCENERY ABOVE BRADWELL **PHOTO:** *ANDY HEADING*

Bradwell Circuit – Hope Valley

Introduction

A great ride on the southern side of the Hope Valley. Although just fitting onto the Dark Peak map, this route is mainly on limestone, so prepare yourself for a little less grip on the rocks beneath your tyres. The drainage is good, so expect it to be in condition all year round.

Incorporating quite a bit of steady mileage, this route also throws in a couple of well scary downhills – and an option to explore the Pin Dale 'Drop Zone'.

The Ride

Starting from Hope, the route warms up nicely along a main road before a gruelling tarmac/gravel ascent up onto Shatton Moor. It then takes a big, wide circle round the Overdale Watershed. The first real descent is a little awkward to spot, but it's well worth finding and drops you, exhilarated, into Bradwell. The next section behind Hope Valley Cement Works is unusual – a bit like mountain biking through the location of a cheap 70s sci-fi series. Then it's steeply up on back roads and around some impressive holes in the ground to meet up with the Limestone Way and, eventually, a very demanding descent through Cave Dale. All that remains now is a little more road work to take you back to Hope.

BRADWELL CIRCUIT	GRADE: ▲»▲
DISTANCE: 17KM	**TOTAL ASCENT:** 752M
START/FINISH: HOPE	**GRID REFERENCE:** 172 835
PARKING: HOPE VILLAGE CAR PARK	**CAFÉ:** WOODBINE CAFÉ Tel: 01433 621 407
PUBLIC HOUSE: TRAVELLERS REST Tel: 01433 620 363	

PHOTO: ANDY HEADING

N

0 miles

0 km   1

P

P

Castl

Speedwell
Cavern

Peak
Cavern

4

Cavedale

3

Hollandtwine
Mine (disused)

Hazard Mine
(disused)

BRADWELL
MOOR

MAP 07

Bradwell Circuit

Directions – Bradwell Circuit

1 R out of **Hope car park** » SA (east) in the direction of Hathersage along A6187 for 2km to R turn at lights onto B6049 follow this for 0.5km to L turn onto Brough Lane, just before narrow road bridge » Up steep hill on tarmac, keep SA onto track where the road bends off » Continue SA through gates to join tarmac road » Follow it L to descend into Shatton » Cross ford then R up steep climb on tarmac » Long climb to gate, then follow walled track past mast » Bear L over more eroded tracks, soon curving back R past road head curving around Overdale Watershed » Good track starts to descend – look out for gate on L (with old rusty latch) after 0.5km (easy to miss) » L through gate, diagonally across field on small track to gate » Through gate, keep R along wall, bear L for good, exciting descent into Bradwell » Keep R, turn R onto B6049

2 Descend through village, through lights, after 0.5km fork L onto Town Lane, just before football field » SA at cross roads up track to gate, then R down path onto bridleway leading down into quarry » Keep SA at all junctions following waymarks leading across quarry roads » Stay with this bridleway to its end at road » Turn L, climb steeply up track past Pin Dale Quarry (Motocross playground all around you here. Some good drop offs, jumps etc. to be had, but handle with care!) » Turn R at top, turn L onto road » Follow road up past LH bend, turn R onto wide Dirtlow Rake track just before cattle grid

3 Follow track parallel to road then up and away from road » SA along track past large quarry on R » SA through gate » At bridleway crossroads, take track through gate on R » Follow track across field signposted *Castleton*, bearing down and slightly R towards small gate in drystone wall (**ignore 4WD tracks leading off up SA**) » Through gate, follow track down and L into Cavedale, keeping wall on L to gate » Through gate, track becomes very steep and very rocky (full-on trials skills required for success!), eventually easing as dale opens out, continue SA to gate

4 Through gate, R up road to acute fork » Take L fork, slightly up then down to junction, bear L, continue SA crossing railway cutting » Bear L over stream into Hope » Bear L for **car park** ⬢OR⬢ Take R fork, follow road steeply uphill to L turn for descent of Pin Dale » From base of Pin Dale continue SA crossing railway cutting » Bear L over stream into Hope » Bear L for **car park**

A RAPID DESCENT TO STRINES STATION **PHOTO:** *JOHN HOULIHAN*

Disley Circuit – West Peak

Introduction

More of a big loop around New Mills, this circuit uses a cunningly linked network of bridleways – mainly consisting of rocky farm tracks – to take in a variety of superb terrain. With the emphasis on climbing, this route is a very good test of fitness.

The Ride

From Disley Station (various parking) this route climbs out above the town, soon dropping down into the congested Goyt Valley, before climbing back up to Chinley Churn where commanding views of the entire route can be enjoyed. We then drop into and climb out of the Sett Valley before the route swings north, contouring around New Mills. An excellent descent follows back into the Goyt Valley and then another climb returns you to Disley.

DISLEY CIRCUIT   GRADE: ▲»▲

DISTANCE: 22KM
START/FINISH: DISLEY
PARKING: DISLEY STATION CAR PARK
PUBLIC HOUSE: THE FOX INN Tel: 0161 427 1634

TOTAL ASCENT: 855M
GRID REFERENCE: 997 854
CAFÉ: BRING SANDWICHES!

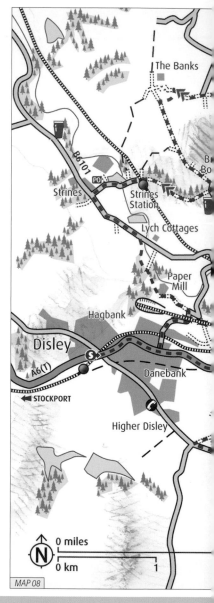

trail tips

2 Warm Up

You'll get better value out of a ride if you spend a few minutes warming up before you hit any tough stuff. We recommend some gentle stretching and a 5–10 minute coast at about 30–50% of maximum effort to get the muscles working before they build up too much lactic. How you do this is as much about your personal preferences as sports science, but for more advice on warming up visit our web-site:

www.**v-graphics**.co.uk

PHOTO: ANDY HEADING

MAP 08

Disley Circuit

Directions – Disley Circuit

1 Leaving **Disley Station car park**, head E out of the town centre on the busy A6 for 1.25km **»** Turn R up Greenshall Lane (track just past & opposite Little Chef), hard climbing, initially on very loose, rocky surface then farm track for 1km to meet road at top **»** Turn L on road for 2km, passing Easter Cottage on R to unsigned doubletrack bridleway through gate on L **»** Descend bridleway to Furness Vale, passing Diglee Farm, continue SA along farm track to join tarmac **»** Turn L at bottom to meet A6 **»** Cross busy A6, SA past station, continue descent on tarmac to take sharp R turn on tarmac as road starts to ascend after Goyt bridge

2 After 0.5km take signposted bridleway L (a little way past railway bridge, on bend in road) **»** Take LH fork, follow doubletrack then rocky path on R, just past Howcroft Farm – a steady climb – to meet road **»** L descend steeply on tarmac to signposted bridleway on R **»** SA past cottage on L **»** SA through gate climb easily up grassy track through fields, stream on L **»** Go through gate through Hollinhurst Head Farm, continue SA up to meet main track at Moor Lodge

3 Turn L, fast descent past quarry on R to Birch Vale **»** Turn R on main road to cut back L opposite The Grouse (in the direction of Thornsett) **»** Cross River Sett, then take bridleway on R – stiff climb on a variety of surfaces takes you up to road

PHOTO: JOHN HOULIHAN

4 Turn L , climb up steeply for 400m to brow of hill **»** Turn R past quarry onto farm track **»** Pass farm with lots of barking dogs **»** Take first bridleway on L (signposted *No Motor Vehicles Except for Access by Agricultural Vehicles*) – initially a grassy doubletrack through gate, then very pleasant descent down walled path joining tarmac to pass Aspenshaw Hall **»** Continue SA downhill at road junction then make steep tarmac climb past Lydiate Farm and Blake Hall on R for 1km **»** Turn L up rocky bridleway (opposite Briargrove Farm), follow this, mainly uphill, to road **»** Turn R on tarmac, then almost immediately L to follow rocky track along edge of woods to four-way junction **»** Continue SA along track **»** After 0.75km take track to L (Black Lane) **»** Follow this to its end (currently very loose) at a three-way junction with farm tracks just below large cross up and L **»** SA at junction, metalled road soon becomes bumpy – continue past a couple of posh dwellings on L & ignore L turn – bumpy track continues downhill and curves LW (next to golf course on R), follow very loose path steeply downwards just R of where track turns L into dwelling, then almost immediately L through gateway – track stays very loose as it drops down and out at T-junction past more posh dwellings **»** Got that? Phew! Turn L to join fairly rocky track and fast descent **»** Ignore acute R turn where rocky track meets better surface, climb up SA, then make short descent into Brook Bottom, turn R then L past Fox Inn (yes, it is an excellent pub)

5 Turn R, just after pub, to follow wide track (signposted *Goyt Way*) – excellent fast descent past Strines Station (alternative start) **»** SA down road past lake on R and over bridge to reach junction with B6101 **»** L along road for 1km to take bridleway on R (this is a small path just past private road, opposite Lych Cottage, just before bridge) **»** Muddy path leads along river, past paper mill to reach road out of mill – RW up tarmac road, turn R under railway track, continue climbing over canal, under second railway bridge to A6 **»** R along A6 back to **Disley Station car park**

LADYBOWER CLASSIC & FIGURE OF 8

GRADE: ▲»▲

DISTANCE: CLASSIC: 20KM   FIGURE OF 8: +14KM   **TOTAL ASCENT:** CLASSIC: 758M   FIGURE OF 8: +496M

START/FINISH: LADYBOWER RESERVOIR   **GRID REFERENCE:** 203 860

ALTERNATIVE START/FINISH: FAIRHOLMES PICNIC SITE AND CAR PARK **GRID REFERENCE:** 174 893

PARKING: HEATHERDENE CAR PARK, NR. BAMFORD   **CAFÉ:** FAIRHOLMES VISITOR CENTRE Tel: 01433 650 953

PUBLIC HOUSE: LADYBOWER INN Tel: 01433 651 936

MELLOW RIDING, LADYBOWER **PHOTO:** *ANDY HEADING*

Ladybower Classic & Figure of 8
– Upper Derwent

Introduction

This all-time classic is one of the best mtb routes in the Dark Peak. Challenging, technical climbs and exhilarating descents are complimented by brilliant scenery – some of the best that Derbyshire has to offer. Do the **Classic Circuit** for a fantastic short day out, or link into the **Figure of 8** for a bit of an epic. This is a route to savour again and again, as subtle intricacies of line unravel themselves and you work your way to a clean run – which would be no mean achievement.

Get on it this weekend

The Ride

After a barely noticeable road section, the route warms up with a long and teasing climb up on to the Derwent Moors, this takes in a variety of surfaces and an intense stream crossing. The views improve with each easily-won contour, then you take the plunge into one of the best, most varied singletrack descents in the country: taking in bomb-holes, a devilish rutted roller coaster and some tricky rock steps. All you need for the perfect

experience is three cunningly positioned helpers to open the gates! Cruise from here into Fairholmes for a draughty brew stop before tackling the slippery and tough climb up from Gores Farm. After a more sedate but still interesting track, the route plummets into the Hagg Farm descent, one of Derbyshire's premium downhills – bermed, loose, rocky and again, who's turn is it to open that gate on the way down? After carefully crossing the A57, the route then follows the south side of Ladybower for a mellow cool down on some picturesque hard-track.

The **Figure of 8** loop departs from here and cunningly uses back roads and another tasty climb to bring you up onto the gloriously exposed whaleback of Win Hill. 360° panoramas can be enjoyed here on some quality singletrack before dropping down from Hope Cross into another beast of a downhill before finishing with another mellow trip along the south side of Ladybower.

trail tips

3 Eco-Riding

To prevent our precious trails becoming 'wider than the M25', we recommend that we all avoid cutting off 'to the side' and ride as close to the centre of the existing track as possible. In this way we improve our skills – especially when it comes to dealing with mud – and lessen our impact on surrounding vegetation and habitats.

PHOTO: ANDY HEADING

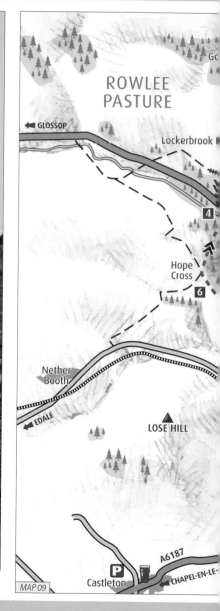

ROWLEE PASTURE

◀ GLOSSOP

Lockerbrook

4

Hope Cross

6

Nether Booth

◀ EDALE

LOSE HILL

A6187

Castleton   CHAPEL-EN-LE-

MAP 09

Reproduced by permission of Ordnance Survey on behalf of The Controller of Her Majesty's Stationery Office. © Crown Copyright. 100025218

N

0 miles — 1

0 km — 1

- - - Classic route
- - - Figure of 8 route

DERWENT VALLEY

Derwent Reservoir

Imes

Jubilee Cottages

Hagg Side

Strines

Strines Resr.

DERWENT MOORS

WHITE TOR

Hurkling Stones

Whinstone Lee Tor

Highshaw Clough

A57

SHEFFIELD →

Cutthroat Bridge

2

Ladybower Inn

ke Pass

Wooler Knoll

Ladybower Reservoir

Heatherdene

5

Bamford Edge

BAMFORD MOOR

WIN HILL

Edge Farm

Aston

Carr Lane

HOPE

Thornhill

HATHERSAGE →

A6013

HATHERSAGE →

Bamford

Ladybower Classic & Figure of 8

DARK PEAK MTB – LADYBOWER CLASSIC & FIGURE OF 8 – UPPER DERWENT – GRADE ▲»▲ 55

Directions – Ladybower Classic & Figure of 8

Classic

1 Leave **Heatherdene car park** and head R on A6013 – cross bridge, head R at lights joining A57 » Head uphill for short distance, looking for Ladybower Inn on L » Immediately past inn, head L up track on fairly rough surface to gate » Through gate, head up R on tricky surface until fork in track – continue SA » Cross moor, trees on R, to intense stream crossing – cross stream, through gate » Cross moor on good track to fork, take L fork » Descend slightly as track curves L above Cutthroat Bridge » Take L fork up for brilliant singletrack ascent » After 1.5km join crossroads (good views from small bluff on L)

2 SA (marked *Bridleway*) to good, testing singletrack below Whinstone Lee Tor – wall on L » Look out for L turn through gate to begin superb, rolling descent » Through gate, follow singletrack with wall on L » Through gate into steep rocky section, cross ford, through large gate to enter courtyard between two ancient barns – look for small gate on L » Drop down steep flagstones, bearing R to gate, straight on here on hard track » Along E edge of Ladybower Reservoir, curve L and cross Mill Brook, soon reaching tarmac road » About 1.5km along this look out for telephone box and Jubilee Cottages » Just past this point follow tarmac road (not track), curving down L below wall of Derwent Dam to reach Fairholmes

3 **(Alternative Fairholmes start)** From **Fairholmes picnic site and car park**, turn right at mini roundabout, head through gates » continue along W side of Derwent Reservoir on tarmac for 1.9km » After Gores Farm, curve L round corner – look out for gate and track leading up sharp L into trees » Continue up track which becomes very steep and slippery in all but the driest of conditions – a notable climb! » Continue up lessening steepness, descend slightly past Lockerbrook Farm » Cross stream and go SA through gate – easy climb for short distance up wider track » 0.4km after farm, track forks » Drop L, through gate into superb descent with bermed corners » Through gate superb descent continues with loose and rocky sections, soon join hard track, drop steeply and **with care** to A57

4 **Cross busy and dangerous A57 with care »** Through gate, down steep and often slippery descent **»** Curve R, cross bridge, continue L and then up track – often very muddy **»** Track forks at gate, L through gate and descend to S bank of Ladybower Reservoir **»** Easily R along track for 5km, finishing with easy climb up hard pack before track curves R and then descends to dam **»** L to cross dam (*note sign asking cyclists to dismount*), join road with cycle track on LH pavement **»** L along road (A6013), R into **Heatherdene car park**

Figure of 8

5 Instead of crossing the dam in **Section 4** above, continue down track (tarmac at first), looking out for permitted bridleway after 0.25km on R **»** Continue SA through two gates to meet road, head R uphill **»** On reaching village of Thornhill, take R turn just before telephone box – Carr Lane (signposted *Not suitable for motors*) **»** Steadily uphill to Aston, through village, after road dips look out for sharp R turn uphill on tarmac (signposted *Win Hill and Hope Cross*) **»** L at Edge Farm **»** Uphill to join muddy walled bridleway **»** Climb track which eventually levels off slightly, undulating beneath the SW flank of Win Hill **»** At ridge summit and junction with wide bridleway, descend L to join sandy track (Roman road), follow this to gate **»** Through gate then short climb to second gate at Hope Cross

6 R here (signposted *Derwent via Hagg*) and descend slightly to gate **»** Through gate into rocky, sunken section, continue descent to next gate **»** Through this and down for superb, very rocky and technical descent – look out for gate on R (junction with **Classic Circuit**) – pause to release bicycle clips and drain out excess adrenalin **»** R through gate and descend to S bank of Ladybower Reservoir **»** Easily R along track for 5km, finishing with easy climb up hard pack before track curves R and then descends to dam **»** L and across dam (*note sign asking cyclists to dismount*), join road with cycle track on LH pavement **»** L along road (A6013), R into **Heatherdene car park**

LADYBOWER 2   GRADE: ▲

DISTANCE: 19KM   **TOTAL ASCENT:** 683M

START/FINISH: LADYBOWER RESERVOIR   **GRID REFERENCE:** 203 860

PARKING: HEATHERDENE CAR PARK, NR. BAMFORD   **CAFÉ:** FAIRHOLMES VISITOR CENTRE Tel: 01433 650 953

PUBLIC HOUSE: LADYBOWER INN Tel: 01433 651 936

ROUGH TERRAIN, CUTTHROAT BRIDGE **PHOTO:** *ANDY HEADING*

Ladybower 2 – Upper Derwent

Introduction

A great complementary route to the **Ladybower Classic / Figure of 8 Circuit** *(see page 52)*. **Though short, this is still a pretty hefty ride with two notable ascents – one is a bit of a chore that gains a lot of height very quickly, the other is a different story and contains a couple of rocky sections that will test the best – especially in the (usual!) damp conditions. The reward for all this effort is access to two spectacular sections of high moorland singletrack that roll on for ages.**

Downhillers will be delighted with two very fast sections of premium gravity action – the satisfyingly long, fast and exciting descent to Gores Farm and a grand swoop down from Derwent Edge.

The Ride

Though this route starts with a pretty gruelling uphill, the rewards are soon gained as you pass through Crookhill Farm and the view opens out across to the spectacular Derwent Moors. The ascent continues, all very grassy but not too demanding, with the outlook improving with each pedal stroke – then the trail drops down *via* some great singletrack, eventually joining a series of sandy ruts that are a blast to ride! After a brief levelling in the terrain, the trail turns right past Lockerbrook Farm and a short rocky climb leading into a rip-roaring descent through the woods on the shore of Derwent Reservoir.

A quick stint on road follows, then it's up up up onto the moors that were tantalisingly glimpsed earlier on. This climb is in stages, divided up by the gates – see how many stages you can ride, it's one of the Peak's great challenges to master all three! Emerging from the top gate, it's back onto the middle ring for an exhilarating singletrack section that takes in some tricky bomb holes before rounding the col for a real treat – a full 1km of superb singletrack descent. Watch out for the boggy section at the bottom!

And there's more to come – this great little route is rounded off with a nice dollop of rocky descent, including a very tricky ford crossing, before we rejoin the A57 and roll back into the car park.

trail tips

4 Horse-Sense

Horses can be nervous. If frightened they may bolt, rear or kick, which could easily result in injury to the rider of the horse or the rider of your bike! Always yield to horse and rider. When approaching from the front, there's less chance of spooking the horse as it will see you coming – just slow down, stop at a safe distance, pull off a little to one side of the trail and allow the horse and rider to pass before getting back on your bike. When approaching from behind, the horse is more likely to hear you before the rider and may react. Unfamiliar sounds such as loud, grinding gear changes are a no-no, but it's good to make a friendly greeting at a sensible volume. When the rider is aware of your presence they will usually stop – then it's a simple matter to pass slowly at a sensible distance.

PHOTO: ANDY HEADING

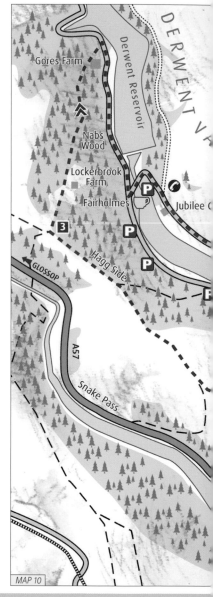

MAP 10

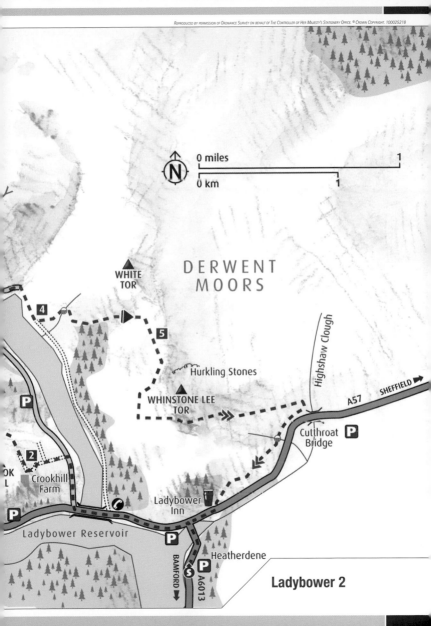

0 miles   1

N

0 km   1

DERWENT
MOORS

WHITE
TOR

4

5

Highshaw Clough

Hurkling Stones

WHINSTONE LEE
TOR

A57   SHEFFIELD

2

Cutthroat
Bridge   P

Crookhill
Farm

Ladybower
Inn

P

Ladybower Reservoir

P

BAMFORD

Heatherdene

P

A6013

Ladybower 2

Directions – Ladybower 2

1 Head R out of **Heatherdene car park**, crossing bridge to lights **»** Turn L across viaduct then R again up road on L (W) bank of reservoir, look out for very steep tarmac road on L after 0.5km (signed *Crookhill Farm*) **»** Up and through Crookhill Farm, keep R of farm house, through gate and R onto track **»** Follow track R

2 Follow RH wall, ignore all tracks that fork L **»** Through gate, follow wall for approx. 100m then bear L to cross exposed moorland – follow wooden marker posts towards gate **»** SA through gate and up through field (signposted *Bridleway to Rowlee Farm and Lockerbrook*) to gate **»** SA through gate, easy riding following wooden stakes to another gate **»** SA through gate, fast descent with woods on R to double gates **»** Ignore bridleway leading R, SA through gates **»** Follow interesting sand and gravel track for 1km to gate and junction with larger track **»** Follow track uphill to junction with good track

3 Go R along gravel road (SA), descend slightly as road curves R to Lockerbrook Farm **»** SA through gate, follow rocky track initially up and then down (increasingly fast!) into the trees **»** Continue descent past awkward RH hairpin to gate **»** Through gate to join tarmac, turn R **»** Follow tarmac SA for 2.25km, eventually reaching mini roundabout near **Fairholmes (alternative starting point)** – take third (last) exit L towards base of dam (beware mosquitoes!) **»** Pass the impressive dam wall of Derwent Reservoir on L – follow road as it curves round up R passing Jubilee Cottages and telephone box **»** About 2.25km of tarmac leads across Mill Brook, look out for gate and bridleway leading up flagstones across a field (signed *Footpath Derwent Edge to Moscar*)

4 Through gate, follow flagstones, climb becomes increasingly tough past cobbled section up to gate **»** Through gate, turn R past two old barns **»** Pass through open gateway, ford stream, up through gate into steep rocky path with wall on R **»** Climb up (very technical and steep) to second gate **»** SA through gate and out into open section, follow obvious rutted track less steeply uphill to gate **»** SA through gate onto open moor, continue SA uphill, initially flat then steep and technical to gate **»** Through gate, turn R onto rough track – engage middle ring!

5   Follow rough track past a few boggy bomb-holes, eventually emerging onto good viewpoint after approx. 1km **»** Follow track SA as it swoops down across open moorland – excellent views **»** Just past boggy section, track curves R next to stream – soon after this take R turn at junction (slightly uphill) **»** Continue SA, joining up with woodland on L **»** Continue through awkward gate to forge stream with care! **»** Make good descent on rocky track to gate on L **»** Through gate, fast descent to A57 and Ladybower Inn **»** Turn R carefully onto A57 **»** Take next L at lights, cross bridge back to **Heatherdene car park**

PHOTO: *ANDY HEADING*

ON THE FLANKS OF MAM TOR **PHOTO:** *ANDY HEADING*

Mam Tor Figure of 8 – Hope Valley

Introduction

Good, short route making the most of the sensational riding along the ridge that connects Mam Tor with Rushop Edge. Two out of the four significant climbs are made on tarmac, the other two are off-road and only really steep in short, rideable sections. Play your cards right – in good, dry conditions this whole route should be manageable without a foot down by the fit rider.

There's a challenge!

The Ride

Out of Castleton and up *via* the wrinkled, collapsing tarmac below Odin's Mine. After some easy road-work, we pass through the gate and climb up onto Rushop Edge to enjoy some spectacular scenery – on a quiet day this can be just magical! Crossing remote ground near the end of the ridge brings us to Chapel Gate – a fast descent of great character – do you dare commit to the high, exposed ridges of decaying tarmac or do you rattle on down the stony ruts? Another road climb then ensues, bringing us stalwartly to the soaring singletrack up and over the shoulder of Mam Tor. Then it's quickly down to Hollins Cross. All that remains from here is to keep focussed for a hair raising descent taking us pretty well back to the car. It's all over much to soon.

MAM TOR FIGURE OF 8	GRADE: ▲
DISTANCE: 15KM	**TOTAL ASCENT:** 628M
START/FINISH: CASTLETON	**GRID REFERENCE:** 149 830
PARKING: CASTLETON CAR PARK	**CAFÉ:** COTTAGE CAFÉ Tel: 01433 670 293
PUBLIC HOUSE: PLENTY TO CHOOSE FROM IN CASTLETON	

5 Pre-ride Check

Best done before you leave the house, not while standing in the car park.

Check:

- tyres for correct pressure;
- all bolts to make sure nothing has worked loose – pay particular attention to head set and quick releases on front and rear wheels;
- brake pads;
- chain lube;
- saddle height.

PHOTO: *JOHN HOULIHAN*

0 miles

0 km   1

Upper Booth

Barbe Booth

P

Chapel Gate Track

LORD'

Rushup Edg

← CHAPEL-EN-LE-FRITH

MAP 11

HOPE

Nether Booth

River Noe

Edale

EDALE

Cottage Cafe

LOSE HILL

DALE OF EDALE

VALE OF EDALE

Greenlands

Hollins Cross

3

MAM TOR

Training & Conference Centre

HATHERSAGE

2

Hollowford Road

Blue John Cavern

Treak Cliff Cavern

A6187

Castleton

Winnats Pass

Speedwell Cavern

Peak Cavern

B6061

BUXTON

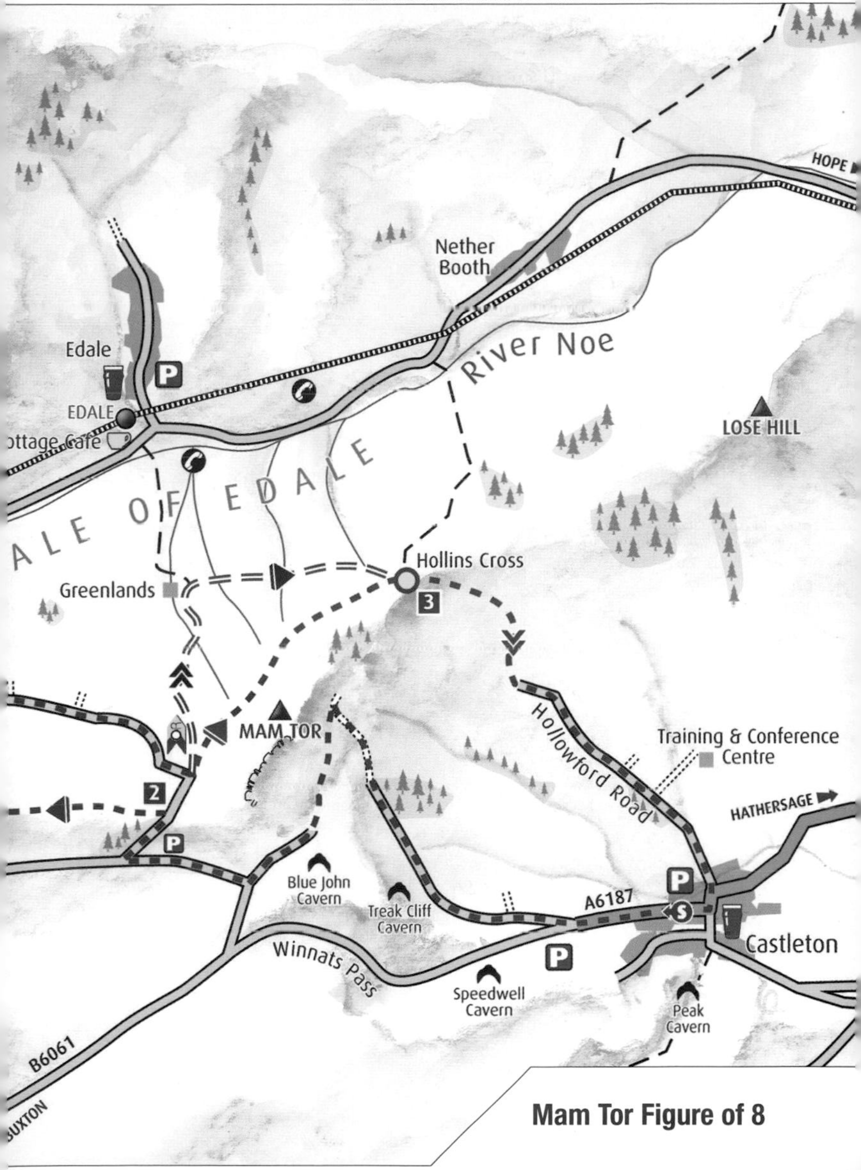

Mam Tor Figure of 8

Directions – Mam Tor Figure of 8

1 L out of **Castleton car park**, follow A6187 out of Castleton **ignoring L turn** uphill to Winnats Pass » SA past Treak Cliff Cavern » Continue SA past bus turning area and up on steep tarmac through gate » Continue up collapsing tarmac road to gate at top – watch out for drop offs! » Continue along short stretch of road to join main road, turn R » Follow road for 0.5km, turn R steeply uphill just past parking area » Follow road up, look out for gate on L

2 Through gate (signposted *Rushop Edge*), begin tough climb » Continue climb passing through gate then up onto Rushop Edge, continue SA along vague level track through several gateways – always keeping wall to right – until path swerves R through gate » Through gate descend L to fork in path » Take R fork (signposted *To Edale Via Barber Booth*), following superb exposed track across moorland, soon descending with great interest *via* broken track with decaying tarmac ridges » Keep on this track through gate to meet road at bottom » R up road, uphill for 1.5km, look out for wooden gate on L by bus stop (almost at 'Col') » Through gate,  continue SA uphill on good singletrack » Continue over shoulder into descent to gate, once through gate continue SA on stone flags through second gate to four-way path junction (Hollins Cross)

3 SA past Hollins Cross, head uphill slightly looking out for blue bridleway arrow pointing off to RH side off main track » Follow fork to narrow gate, through to second gate – cross hillside, path forks R » Follow path R onto sunken path to meet gate at bottom » Through gate, down rocky singletrack to join Hollowford Road » Follow tarmac SA (ignore R turn to Conference Centre), join A6187 » Turn R into **Castleton car park**

▶▶OptionalRoute▶ A demanding alternative. This option adds a scary downhill and a gruelling climb – both officially do-able, both very challenging.

Just past gate, bear L down stony shoot to gate » Through gate into steep, rutted descent, eventually leading to another gate, through this and descend quickly to gate by road and dwelling (Greenlands) » Do not pass through gate, continue SA, initially on pleasant gravel singletrack » Commence climb, which continues with increasing difficulty up through two gates, then into particularly challenging section up to crossroads (Hollins Cross).

TESTING GRADE ON DOCTOR'S GATE **PHOTO:** ANDY HEADING

Snake Doctor – West Peak

Introduction

Short and very, very sharp would be the best way to describe this route. Very useful as an afternoon training route if you're local to the area, this route will test both uphill endurance and, even more, your ability to handle a potentially very dangerous descent!

The Ride

After a fairly prolonged warm up crossing the notorious Pennine byway of the Snake Pass, this route cuts off into the midst of nowhere *via* the course of an ancient road. Tough, technical climbing is followed by an even tougher descent that will initially require full-on trials skills for success – approach with caution. The trail then gradually eases, finishing with a super-fast run on a good track back to civilisation (well, Glossop).

SNAKE DOCTOR	GRADE: ▲»▲
DISTANCE: 16KM	**TOTAL ASCENT:** 524M
START/FINISH: GLOSSOP	**GRID REFERENCE:** 035 943
PARKING: GLOSSOP RAILWAY STATION CAR PARK	**CAFÉ:** PACK SOME GRUB
PUBLIC HOUSE: RELY ON YOUR WATER BOTTLE	

PHOTO: ANDY HEADING

WATCH THAT SPEED PHOTO: ANDY HEADING

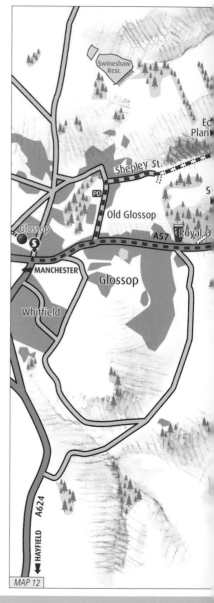

MAP 12

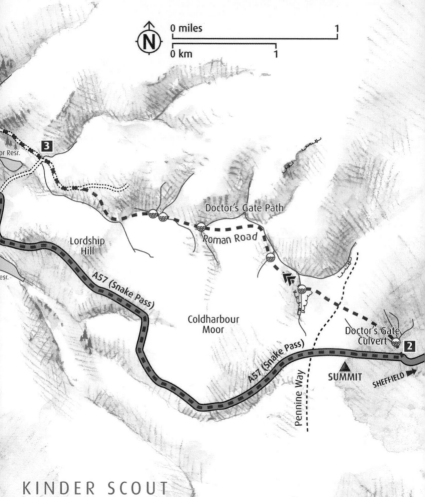

BLEAKLOW

N

0 miles   1

0 km   1

3

or Resr.

Doctor's Gate Path

Roman Road

Lordship
Hill

A57 (Snake Pass)

esr.

Coldharbour
Moor

A57 (Snake Pass)

Doctor's Gate
Culvert   **2**

SUMMIT   SHEFFIELD

Pennine Way

KINDER SCOUT

Snake Doctor

Directions – Snake Doctor

1 **Glossop Railway Station car park »** R out of car park, L at traffic lights onto Sheffield Road (A57) in the direction of the Snake Pass **»** Follow this (usually) very busy road through some good scenery, mainly uphill, for 8km, passing the Pennine Way footpath after 7km **»** After a descent of approx. 1km, look out for bridleway beginning from layby on L (signposted *Doctor's Gate*)

2 SA through gate, follow track to cross ford **»** SA along paving flag track to four way cross roads **»** SA to descend very rough track (Roman road), very technical at first, keep river on R **»** SA down track which eases slightly but continues to throw in some very difficult sections **»** After approx. 3km from cross roads, and after crossing river twice, join smooth, fast track to gate **»** Through gate, take RH bridge (ignore L which leads to farm)

3 After 2.3km and another gate, track turns near some works into Shepley Street **»** Follow Shepley Street to T-junction **»** Turn L past post office, follow road to T-junction **»** Turn R onto A57 **»** Downhill for 0.5km to four way junction at **Glossop Railway Station**, turn R into car park

PHOTO: *ANDY HEADING*

WHARNCLIFFE

GRADE:

DISTANCE: APPROX 12KM

TOTAL ASCENT: DEPENDENT ON LAPS

START/FINISH: WHARNCLIFFE WOODS

GRID REFERENCE: 325 950

PARKING: WHARNCLIFFE WOODS FORESTRY COMMISSION CAR PARK

CAFÉ: POWER BAR ESSENTIAL

PUBLIC HOUSE: CHECK OUT GRENOSIDE

EXPERIENCE THE BUZZ - WHARNCLIFFE SINGLETRACK **PHOTO:** *JOHN HOULIHAN*

Wharncliffe – Sheffield

Introduction

Welcome to South Yorkshire's downhill mecca!

Something completely different, this is a variation on the existing way-marked Black Route trail that misses out a couple of nasty overgrown sections and adds in a couple of the more accessible downhills for good measure.

The trail surface at Wharncliffe consists of dug out dirt, great in dry conditions, but it soon turns into the gloopiest mud imaginable when wet.

We recommend that you plan your visit to Wharncliffe for the drier summer months when the downhills will be at their fastest and the uphills at there most 'do-able'. This approach will also help to maintain the trails. There are also two official, waymarked routes in Wharncliffe:

Black: A tough cross-country route that has some brutal climbs and a few sections that may be a little overgrown with brambles (this situation may improve with traffic) – otherwise recommended if you're skills are up to it.

Green: Easy forest road stuff.

Note on Access: Things appear to be fairly easy going at Wharncliffe, but the presence of tyre tracks doesn't mean that there is a right of way for mountain bikers *(see pages viii – x)* Please stick to way-marked trails until you've got the local knowledge of what does and doesn't 'go'. Updates on the current situation in the woods can be gained from the Recreation Rangers: **01623 822 447**

The Ride

A fast descent from the car park soon joins up with the way-marked Black Route for a short section of testing singletrack. Soon you pop back out of the woods for a quick descent on forest roads, leading back onto the black circuit for more testing singletrack – including a technical, rutted climb. Heading off left from here, the black circuit continues along fire roads before nipping back into the woods. After you've completed this section (which brings you to the top of Wharncliffe's notorious downhills) we recommend heading left for a great descent and follow our directions to describe a very cool series of loops connecting some good downhills before returning to the car park. This makes for a very memorable 'downhill lite' kind of afternoon – but we still recommend that you handle it with care (especially on first acquaintance).

MAP 13

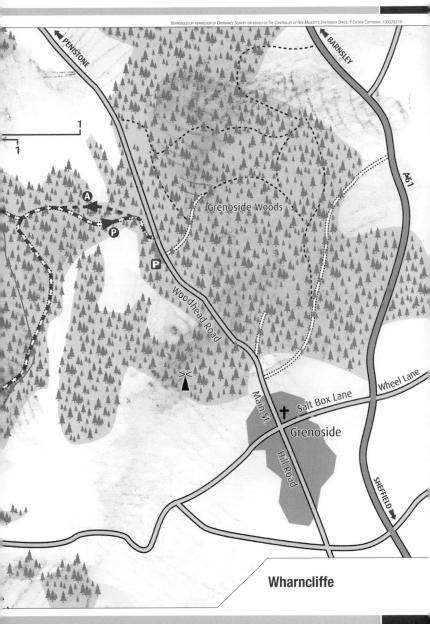

Wharncliffe

From **Wharncliffe Woods Forestry Commission car park**, head SA downhill past barrier on Forestry Commission road (signposted *No Admittance to Unauthorised Vehicles*) ignore track almost immediately on R (opposite Trans Pennine Trail notice on L) – look out for Black Route waymark pointing into woods on R, just after second barrier **»** **A –** Follow singletrack down through woods and back onto forest road, turn R back onto forest road following Black Route waymark – continue, mostly in descent down forest road **»** Bear R at junction following Black Route waymark, road curves LW past small pond on L **»** Turn R at next junction following Black Route waymark, **B –** look out for discrete Black Route waymark on L just past area of new planting, this leads out *via* a superb section of singletrack across open ground **»** Continue to follow Black Route waymarks into woods, across sandy track, then back into woods, soon bearing R to cross stream and climb out again **»** Follow RW fork at path junction just past stream, continue along singletrack which meets overgrown forest track and turns R uphill at Black Route waymark **C –** (very rutted – desperate in the wet!) **»** At junction with forest road turn L at Black Route waymark, descending quickly **»** Look out for Black Route waymark pointing R into woods across tiny bridge, follow this along singletrack section through woods, cross track past **D –** Black Route waymark to junction with forest road

Wharncliffe Downhills begin here...

On rejoining forest track, ignore Black Route waymark and turn L looking out for Black Route waymark pointing down steep downhill (part of the Black Route but now out of sequence!) **»** Turn R for steep downhill, initially quite rocky **E –** **»** Continue downhill, take R where path forks and 'chutes' down into woods, **F –** eventually joining up with forest track at bottom. **Take care!**

Turn L on forest road and continue past junction with Trans Pennine Trail, **G –** dropping then climbing slightly to electricity pylon that nearly touches forest road on your L – look out for discrete Black Route waymark on R **»** Turn L and up beneath electricity pylon **H –** to follow tight singletrack through trees, eventually bearing R at track junction to follow Black Route waymark steeply uphill **I –** (soon joining point at which you originally cut off R on your descent!) **»** Climb continues, easing for a bit before becoming really vicious near the top!

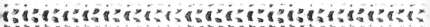

Get your breath back and head L along forest track (opposite direction to Black Route waymark), passing grassy track on R, rocky outlook on L and enticing looking trail leading steeply down into the woods – what you are looking for is an old fire road that comes up acutely from the L and is easy to miss (there is currently a boulder on top and to L) **»** Descend LW down steep and loose ground **J –** to rejoin forest road at bottom **»** Turn R, follow forest road past a couple of downhill run-outs and, eventually, an oozy red stream **K –** to junction with track coming down from R (ignore forest road signposted *Wortley* SA) **»** R up track, R again at junction by pylon, head up steep and loose forest road **L – »** Continue SA where track levels, past the two descents you made earlier – track then descends slightly to junction – continue SA **»** Continue fast descent, **M –** eventually reaching Black Route waymark near junction **»** Follow this R for very technical downhill **N – take care!**

At junction with forest road turn L uphill (Black Route waymark) **»** At next junction continue LW, steeply up forest track following sign for *Trans Pennine Trail Sheffield* (ignore Black Route waymark pointing R), past another sign for *Trans Pennine Trail Sheffield* – ignore track leading down R **»** Continue to fork, take R fork up and R (follow Black Route waymark) **»** Continue SA where track almost doubles back **»** SA at junction on well surfaced forest road, **O –** eventually passing bridleway sign pointing R – ignore this – continue SA to junction with path by small bridge – follow forest track LW (following Green Route & Black Route waymarks) **»** Turn R at large junction (signposted *Trans Pennine Trail Sheffield* & Black Route waymark) continue uphill on gravel track **P –** to **Wharncliffe Woods Forestry Commission car park**

If you're still keen check out the 'skills' area in the woods over to the right (if you're looking down the forestry commission road) of the car park – lots of urban-style fun: drop offs, jumps and more.

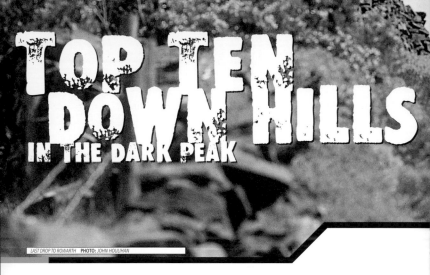

TOP TEN DOWNHILLS IN THE DARK PEAK

Graded on both quality and difficulty. We recommend a tough XC full-susser for maximum riding pleasure. It goes without saying that the utmost care should be taken on these downhills – ride with aptitude rather than attitude.

1   Cave Dale Starting out benignly enough, this limestone horror only reveals its true colours about two-thirds of the way down, just through a little gate. The intimidating, toothy, nettle infested rocky gully that is the only way down will make most riders keen to stay off the bike and start walking. Stay confident, keep the momentum going and easy with that front brake - you may just survive!

2   Mam Tor – True Downhill From the gate on Cold Side (just below Mam Nick) a steep, stony shoot leads down to a second gate. The track past this becomes steep, rutted and twists alarmingly to create a nightmare of off-camber ridges. Top Tip - stick to your line choices.

3   The Beast of Hope Cross From Hope Cross, this great descent consists of three increasingly difficult sections divided by two gates. From the second gate all hell breaks loose.
Top Tips - best to attack the hairpin half way down by crossing it at a 45° angle, and keep your concentration up in the closing stages – it stays loose right to the end.

4   Derwent Edge The descent from the gate at 376m is a classic downhill experience – a real corker that is delightfully varied and only marred by the presence of three gates that interrupt the force of gravity. Starting with a classy, rolling, rutted section to gate number one, the descent then turns into a fast section of rutted singletrack. Through the next two gates, the downhill chutes into increasingly rocky territory - culminating in a series of testing mini rock steps.

check out www.v-graphics.co.uk for detailed information & co-ordinates

5 **Wharncliffe – 1st descent** Quintessentially Wharncliffe – steep, fast and littered with obstacles! From the black waymark on the forest road, follow the short, steep, rocky and rooty chute down into the woods. A smoothish section of very fast track then leads past a couple of serious looking jumps, out briefly into the open, and then curves steeply back down into the gloom where things get tight and twisted.

6 **Hagg Farm** Not a long descent, but a very good one. Short drop to gate then tricky, bermed surface to second gate and down into the woods. Don't relax, the temptingly fast gradient still throws in plenty of loose stuff and some awkward rock steps – you could be eating dirt here. Often slippy.

7 **Gores Farm** The descent proper starts around Lockerbrook. This one starts out straight and turbo fast, with plenty of opportunities to catch air over the numerous drainage bars that crisscross the track. Things then get pretty rocky as the descent drops into the woods and past a critical hair pin.

8 **Cumberland Brook** An unusual and fairly out of the way descent this one - never overly steep, but good and long. The track starts with a fast, smooth section before things get really loose down past a sharp bend. Sustained concentration essential!

9 **Last Drop to Rowarth** A real bone-shaker!

10 **Mam Tor – Hollins Cross Left Hand** Is this a top-ten downhill? We think it just qualifies thanks to the steep, technical, rock-step introduction that sets the pace right from the start. Increasingly smooth and flowing as the steepness relents, don't get caught out by the deep ruts and adverse cambers that keep things interesting throughout.

Enduros

sponsored by **GORE**
BIKE·WEAR

www.gorebikewear.com

SECTION 3

Enduros

Enduros

Challenging rides for fit and experienced mountain bikers.
Never to be undertaken lightly, an enduro will demand
endurance (no surprise there), tenacity, skill and
self-sufficiency. Taking you well into the Dark Heart of
the Dark Peak – enduros offer the essence of 'real' mountain
biking and cover some exceptional terrain. Come prepared.

BUXTON

GRADE: ▲ »

DISTANCE: 25KM   OPTIONAL LOOP: +15KM

TOTAL ASCENT: 827M   OPTIONAL LOOP: 509M

START/FINISH: BUXTON

GRID REFERENCE: 058 737

PARKING: BUXTON PAY & DISPLAY CAR PARK (RAILWAY STATION)

CAFÉ: FIVEWAYS CAFÉ, JUNCTION OF DALE ROAD/LONDON ROAD/HIGH STREET Tel: 0129 872 018

PUBLIC HOUSE: CAT AND FIDDLE Tel: 0129 823 364

WOODLAND CRUISING, GOYT VALLEY **PHOTO:** *JOHN HOULIHAN*

Buxton – West Peak

Introduction

A superb, scenic excursion into the gritstone hills of the 'Honorary Dark Peak' around Buxton. The loop around the Goyt Valley is a fine example of what might be described as 'mountain biking lite': testing enough, but rideable all the way for the reasonably fit. The optional loop adds more than a little spice, including an exposed high moorland crossing and a superb, loose and rocky descent that leads into the course of Cumberland Brook.

The Ride

Starting out of the old spa town of Buxton, the route winds up nicely on a long but mellow road section, before kicking off into the moors along the course of Roman road. From here it's a bit of convoluted road-work before you hit the pleasing section of rocky track around Ladder Hill. Crossing the busy A5004 and then the River Goyt, the trail climbs steeply and then cruises steadily through the pleasant and varied countryside of the Goyt Valley. This is all pretty much middle-ring stuff until you make the steep climb out of Mill Clough – quite a challenging ascent, especially in muddy conditions. The trail continues through woodlands before dropping down to the banks of Errwood Reservoir, where a quiet road leads up through some wild looking scenery.

At the roadhead of Derbyshire Bridge, you have the option of cutting the ride short and heading back to Buxton – but it's well worth engaging with the extra mileage.

The longer ride continues along the road to The Cat and Fiddle, which offers a very welcome stop for lunch. Crossing a lethal section of the A537, the route takes a really cool course across the wilderness *via* a rough, flattish bridleway to meet the road, descend a bit and join a really peachy descent that rocks and rolls down to meet the course of Cumberland Brook. From here we take some scenic back-roads up for a short but very worthwhile section of steep descent, then we pay for all the downhill by climbing back up to the A537 – a bit of a slog I'm afraid.

Tarmac takes us back to the roadhead at Derbyshire Bridge, then we head back out into the wilds for one last climb and great finale – the fabulous fast and loose descent back into Buxton.

SHINING TOR

A537

P

Stanley
Arms

Chapel House
✝

8

☕ Peak View House

🍺 Cat & Fiddle

Derbys
Bridg

Macclesfield
Forest

◄ LANGLEY

A537

P

Danebower
Hollow

P

7

Cumberland Brook

Clough
House

A54

◄ CONGLETON

MAP 14

continues on
NEXT PAGE

T'S MOSS

A5004

P

S

A53

Buxton

Burbage

Five-Ways
Cafe

A54

A515

0 miles   1

N

0 km   1

LEEK

Buxton (Part 1)

CROSSING THE GOYT **PHOTO:** *JOHN HOULIHAN*

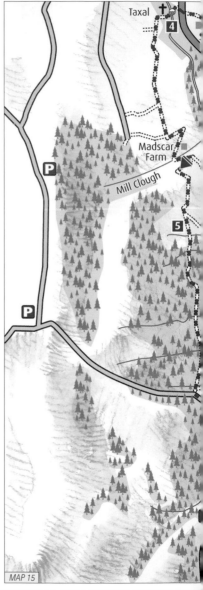

Taxal

Madscar
Farm

Mill Clough

MAP 15

Elnor Lane Farm

Long Lane

Combs Reservoir

LADDER HILL

3 ■ Thorny Lee

Wythen Lache

N
0 miles 1
0 km 1

2 ■ White Hall Centre

continued from
LAST PAGE

Roman Road

Cold Springs Farm

Buxton (Part 2)

Directions – Buxton

1 Turn R out of **Buxton Railway Station** car park, head downhill to first roundabout **»** SA to second roundabout, turn R uphill onto Manchester Road/Longhill Road (A5004) **»** Climb steadily up A5004 for 1.2km to just past Cold Springs Farm, where road bends sharply to L – continue SA onto narrow track (Roman road) **»** Climb up and through gate into shortish technical section, SA out across moorland, descend to White Hall Centre and junction of tracks

2 Ignore doubletrack on L of entrance to White Hall Centre, follow track as it curves down and to R **»** SA along road, ignore road that drops down to R, continue along road over brow of hill **»** Road drops slightly then curves round to R – continue to Wythen Lache farm on R – look out for gate, just to L of farm, leading into walled track **»** Through gate, follow walled track to second gate **»** SA through gate, follow track across field to descend with interest to another gate

3 SA through gate, join tarmac, drop down past Thorny Lee, turn L onto rutted, stony road (Long Lane) where it meets road heading R uphill **»** Follow this track to T-junction with tarmac at Old Road **»** Turn R, roll down Old Road on southern edge of Whaley Bridge, take second L into Shallcross Avenue, follow road up past Shallcross Hall Farm then make good fast descent to meet busy Long Hill (A5004) **with care!**

4 Cross road into large lay-by on opposite side **»** Drop down steep track leading downwards to ford (footbridge on R is the sensible option!) **»** Climb steeply up concrete road on opposite side, through church yard up to Taxal, turn L at top **»** Follow tarmac road climbing gently upwards to reach T-junction overlooking Mill Clough at Overton Hall Farm **»** Turn L for fast, smooth downhill past RH hairpin bend, drop down to gate at Madscar Farm **»** SA through gate and down steeply to cross steam at bottom of Mill Clough **»** Through gate, climb up track for 100m – R through gate just before Knipe Farm **»** Make challenging climb up rutted track to gate **»** SA through gate, follow walled track past roofless barn where track splits – take lower branch SA to Oldfield Farm

5 Continue through farmyard, bear R onto hardpack forest road signposted *Hoo Moor* **»** SA through trees to T-junction with tarmac road, The Street **»** Turn L, roll steeply down road to ride past W side of Errwood Reservoir **»** SA for gradual climb up to Derbyshire Bridge and Visitor Centre

OptionalRoute

6 Turn R past Derbyshire Bridge, continue SA steadily uphill for 1.85km, to turn R onto the very busy A537 near to The Cat and Fiddle » Just opposite the pub, a flattish, hardpack, loose stone bridleway leads L across the moor – follow this to join the A54 » Turn R onto A54, follow this for 1.25km, looking out for bridleway entrance (signposted *Footpath to Cat & Fiddle/Cumberland Brook and Clough House*) on R which meets road at an acute angle and slopes upwards » After a few steep, uphill pedal-strokes, a great descent starts – fast and smooth to sharp L, then rocky down to grassy hollow and junction with footpath near gate » SA through gate, continue steep, loose and rocky descent with great interest to L turn, ford stream near bottom, then through gate to junction with road opposite Clough House

7 Turn R, descend to junction, turn R onto road » Follow road for 2km, past lay-by on L to uphill L turn – turn L steeply uphill on tarmac » Turn first R on tarmac by entrance to forest, follow road to L turn (signposted *Macc. Forest*) on tarmac – turn L uphill » On entering hamlet of Chapel House, head R past church on R to meet bridleway on R where road curves down and L » Turn R onto bridleway for increasingly good, fast descent – take care at the bottom as it meets abruptly with the road.

8 Turn L, roll down hill to T-junction, turn L » Follow road to second T-junction, turn R passing Stanley Arms, following sign to Buxton » Follow road (enthusiastically!) uphill to T-junction with busy A537 » **Cross A537 RW with great care**, continue uphill past tea house on L » SA past The Cat and Fiddle, turn L to descend back on tarmac to Derbyshire Bridge

Finish

9 At Derbyshire Bridge Visitor Centre, turn L off road onto rough track (signposted *Buxton*) » Climb up for a short distance, then make excellent, fast, rocky descent (take care with your speed/line) to join tarmac at Burbage » Continue descent to traffic lights, fork L to roll into Buxton on A53 » SA at two roundabouts to reach **Buxton Railway Station car park**

Cut Gate Special – Upper Derwent

Introduction

One of the best routes in this guide, an unmissable opportunity to traverse this world class mountain bike track twice in one day. Most routes in this guide follow a roughly circular or figure of 8 course. This is something different. A long out and back, with a tasty loop at the end (this can be made even tastier by adding an extra loop at the Ladybower end). Oddly it doesn't feel like you're retracing your steps at all as the terrain is so amazingly varied.

The Ride

After heading out of the car park at Fairholmes, this route warms up nicely by coasting along the eastern side of the Derwent and Howden Reservoirs. After a short, tricky section along the side of Cranberry Clough, the terrain really kicks in with a very stiff climb up past some zig-zags – research suggests that this short section is unrideable! Past the zig-zags, it's back on the bike as the climb becomes more realistic (though still challenging), up out of the gully onto open moorland. Further challenging singletrack leads to a brief respite along some flagstones before another short, killer climb takes you up onto Howden Edge and the beginning of a real theme-park descent! After taking in pretty well every kind of obstacle imaginable – including some scorching stony singletrack – the trail sneaks out of Cut Gate and rolls down through some great moorland before skirting above Langsett Reservoir and retracing tyre marks.

The track in return does have a long hard climb, but it's almost all rideable up to the steep stony section just before the watershed. The terrain stays challenging right up to the cairn at Howden Edge, then it's time to lower your saddle and blast back to Slippery Stones on a truly world class section of trail.

CUT GATE SPECIAL   GRADE: ▲

DISTANCE: 26KM   **TOTAL ASCENT:** 1207M
START/FINISH: FAIRHOLMES/LADYBOWER RESERVOIR
GRID REFERENCE: 173 894   **PARKING:** FAIRHOLMES CAR PARK
CAFÉ: FAIRHOLMES VISITOR CENTRE Tel: 01433 650 953
PUBLIC HOUSE: LADYBOWER INN Tel: 01433 651 241

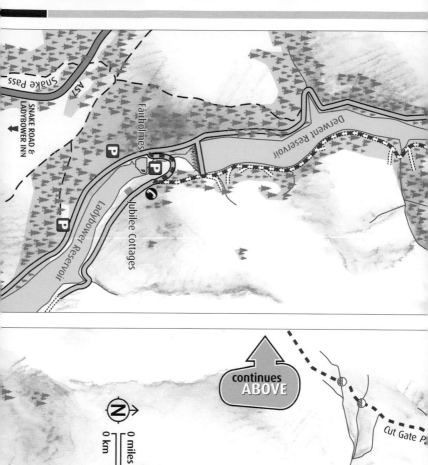

SNAKE ROAD &
LADYBOWER INN

Snake Pass

A57

Fairholmes

Derwent Reservoir

P

P

P

P

Ladybower Reservoir

Jubilee Cottages

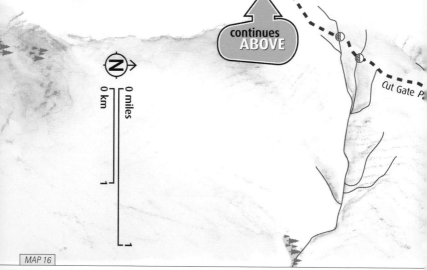

continues
ABOVE

N

0 miles
0 km

1

1

Cut Gate P

MAP 16

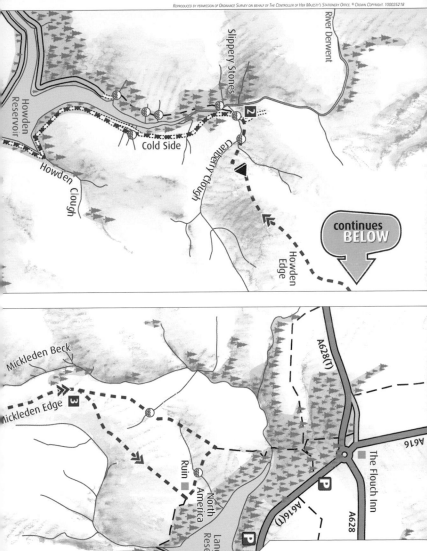

River Derwent

Slippery Stones

Howden Reservoir

Cold Side

Howden Clough

2

Cranberry Clough

continues BELOW

Howden Edge

Mickleden Beck

3

Mickleden Edge

Ruin

North America

Langsett Reservoir

A628(T)

A616

The Flouch Inn

P

A616(T)

P

A628

Cut Gate Special

Directions – Cut Gate Special

1 **Fairholmes car park »** R out of car park, R again at mini roundabout – take second exit through gate, follow tarmac past impressive wall of Derwent Dam on L **»** Follow road as it curves R uphill to junction with tarmac road on R, **»** L at junction (signposted *Bridleway to Slippery Stones*), through gate onto rough track **»** Follow track as it skirts E side of reservoir, eventually heading slightly up and out onto moors before a fast descent drops you down near Slippery Stones (old pack horse bridge down and L)

2 Continue SA (signed *Langsett and Flouch Inn*), ford stream and soon take RH path (ignore track SA – this is a footpath) along L side of stream **»** Continue past second stream crossing, follow RH branch of path (steps on L are a footpath) **»** Climb/push up zig-zags, path soon becomes rideable again (with conviction) out of clough and onto moors **»** Tough singletrack section follows, then flagstones up to short sharp climb to Howden Edge **»** From here trail maintains great interest to join course of stream, followed by loose section and then magical, stony, well defined singletrack **»** After approx 3km from Howden Edge, look out for R turn by sign (signposted *Langsett and Penistone*)

3 Turn R, follow classy moorland singletrack SA, eventually joining up with wall on L – follow this to T-junction at bottom, next to gate leading through to some ruins **»** L through gate and past ruins of North America Farm **»** Follow track slightly upwards to T junction with path coming up from valley floor **»** L along track, more great moorland singletrack leads to short sharp descent before climbing up to meet better defined, stony track of Cut Gate **»** Retrace steps with conviction (mostly rideable, but with a few nasty steps to trip you up!) all the way back to the Cairn at the top of Howden Edge – prepare for supersonic descent! **»** Superb singletrack descent all the way back down past flags etc. into Cranberry Clough – note: take bridleway L by marker just past first set of rock steps **»** Retrace steps past Slippery Stones to **Fairholmes car park**

STEADY CLIMBING UP TO SHATTON MOOR **PHOTO:** ANDY HEADING

Hathersage Circuit – Hope Valley

Introduction

An odd route taking in lots of fast tracks, with fantastic views of high moorland and interesting valley landscapes. Circling the lower Hope Valley, this route is quick going and rewarding, whatever the season.

The Ride

Starting in Hathersage, height is easily won up towards Abney, before contouring round to Offerton Hall. From here superb moorland bridleway makes an easy ascent over Shatton Moor, before a fast and furious descent to Brough. An ascent of Win Hill follows and then it's along the Roman road to the challenging Hope Cross descent. More fast hard pack can be enjoyed along the shore of Ladybower, before dropping into Bamford village and then out again on deteriorating back lanes, to an interesting bridleway dropping back into Hathersage.

HATHERSAGE CIRCUIT	GRADE: ▲
DISTANCE: 29KM	**TOTAL ASCENT:** 1060M
START/FINISH: HATHERSAGE	**GRID REFERENCE:** 232 813
PARKING: HATHERSAGE SWIMMING POOL PAY AND DISPLAY CAR PARK, ODDFELLOWS ROAD	
CAFÉ: OUTSIDE CAFÉ Tel: 01433 651 159	
PUBLIC HOUSE: THE SCOTSMAN'S PACK Tel: 0114 650 253	

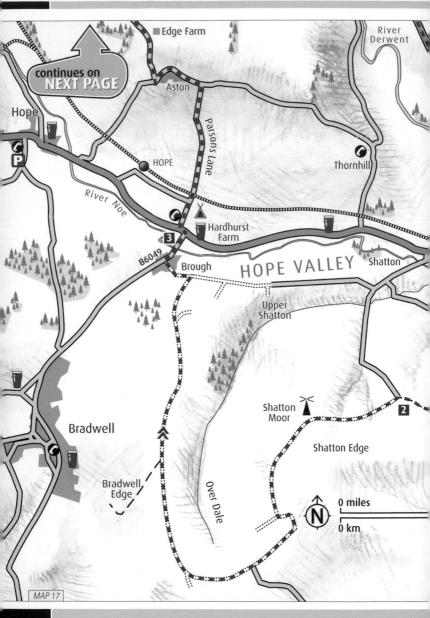

continues on
NEXT PAGE

Edge Farm

River
Derwent

Aston

Hope

HOPE

Parsons Lane

Thornhill

River Noe

Hardhurst
Farm

3

B6049

Brough

HOPE VALLEY

Shatton

Upper
Shatton

Bradwell

Shatton
Moor

2

Shatton Edge

Bradwell
Edge

Over Dale

0 miles

N

0 km

MAP 17

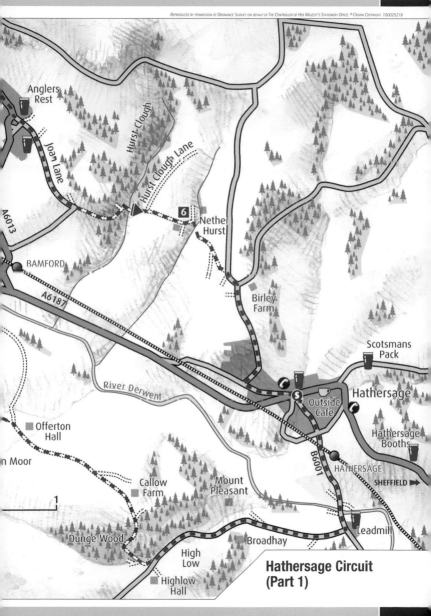

Anglers
Rest

Joan Lane

Hurst Clough

Hurst Clough Lane

6

Nether
Hurst

A6013

BAMFORD

A6187

Birley
Farm

Scotsmans
Pack

River Derwent

Hathersage

Offerton
Hall

n Moor

Outside
Cafe

Hathersage
Booths

Callow
Farm

Mount
Pleasant

HATHERSAGE

B6001

SHEFFIELD ➡

1

Dunge Wood

Broadhay

Leadmill

High
Low

Highlow
Hall

Hathersage Circuit
(Part 1)

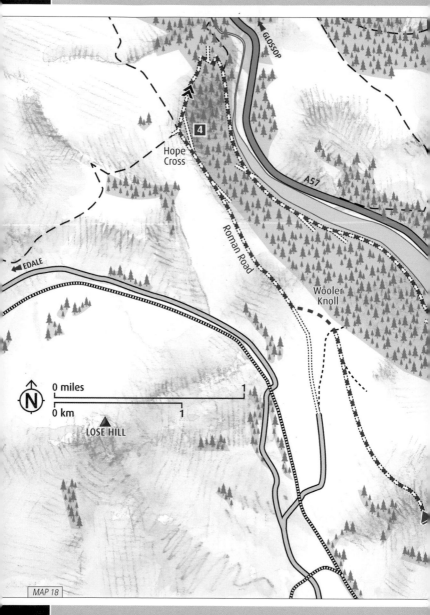

GLOSSOP

A57

4

Hope
Cross

Roman Road

EDALE

Wooler
Knoll

0 miles   1

N

0 km   1

LOSE HILL

MAP 18

DERWENT
MOORS

P

SHEFFIELD ➤
A57

P
Cutthroat
Bridge

ROOK
HILL

P

Ladybower
Inn

Priddock
Wood

Ladybower Reservoir

P Heatherdene

BAMFORD
MOOR

WIN HILL

5

Yorkshire
Bridge

A6013

Lydgate
Farm

continued from
LAST PAGE

ge Farm

**Hathersage Circuit
(Part 2)**

1 R out of **Hathersage swimming pool car park**, then L heading downhill on the B6001 towards Grindleford **»** After just over 1km, take the tarmac road R signed *Gliding Club/Abney* **»** Climb up the road for 1.4km, branching R on the narrow tarmac road just before the farm complex of Highlow Hall on the brow **»** Follow the narrow road, through trees, traversing around the valley head, past Callow House **»** Just before Offerton Hall, at the R bend in the track, go SA on the bridleway across moorland **»** Track narrows and climbs steadily before descent to gate and junction with road

2 L up road and track past mast and along level rutted track onto Shatton Moor **»** At rough T-junction head L on bridleway, following track as it curves round R passing footpath coming from L **»** Pass roadhead on L **»** SA and fast descent – excellent and rocky, becoming tarmac at bottom **»** Follow tarmac curving L to reach main road in Brough

3 R on B6049 to traffic lights **»** L then first R up Parsons Lane to T-junction at Aston **»** L through village **»** After road dips, look out for sharp R turn uphill on tarmac (signposted *Win Hill and Hope Cross*) **»** L at Edge Farm **»** Continue uphill to join muddy walled bridleway **»** Climb track, eventually levelling off slightly, undulating beneath the SW flank of Win Hill **»** At ridge, summit and junction with wide bridleway, descend L to join sandy track (Roman road), follow this to gate **»** Through gate then short climb to second gate at Hope Cross

4 R here (signposted *Derwent via Hagg*) and descend slightly to gate **»** Through gate into rocky, sunken section, continue descent to next gate **»** Through this and down for superb, very rocky and technical descent – look out for gate on R – pause to release bicycle clips and drain out excess adrenalin! **»** R through gate and descend to S bank of Ladybower Reservoir **»** Easily R along track for 5km, finishing with easy climb up hard pack before track curves R and then descends to dam **»** Cross dam (note sign asking cyclists to dismount), join road A6013

5 Turn R, descend into Bamford » In centre of village go L just past the Anglers Rest, SA at crossroads along Joan Lane (keep R at fork) » Where road turns R go SA on road unsuitable for motors – Hurstclough Lane » Ignore L fork at single-bar gate to sewage works » SA to descend into Hurst Clough, get in low gear (you have been warned) for shocking climb out » SA on bridleway where lane turns L

6 Follow bridleway SA through double gates to Nether Hurst, through farm, then SA through gate on bridleway descending to boggy stream » Cross bog, up bridleway » Ignore lane on R keep to bridleway and tackle pleasant, technical climb up narrow slabs through gate, up singletrack to reach tarmac road » R down road to descend into Hathersage » L at T-junction » L then first R on main road, and L into **Hathersage swimming pool car park**

PHOTO: ANDY HEADING

WINTER SUNSHINE IN THE HIGH PEAK **PHOTO:** ANDY HEADING

High Peak Circuit – West Peak

Introduction

A good, demanding, excursion into the western hills of the High Peak. Quite a varied ride, featuring killer climbs and equally killer moorland singletrack. Even though you're never really that far from civilisation, this ride can feel very wild and is tough on the legs – the mileage may not seem like much, but come prepared for a bit of an epic.

The Ride

From Hayfield, the riding warms up easily along the Sett Valley Trail – the course of an old railway. A little easy road-work follows, and then it's up onto the moors *via* a testing ascent to join some absorbing singletrack. After a hefty undulation, the trail climbs steeply up onto the western flank of Kinder Scout before making a fast descent towards Kinder Reservoir and then climbing steeply again (a feature of this route!) onto Middle Moor. Crossing this exciting bit of singletrack (especially at the stream crossing) is perhaps the highlight of the route, but there's still plenty of good riding in store as the road takes you round through Rowarth and across the network of old rock-strewn tracks that leads eventually into Hayfield.

HIGH PEAK CIRCUIT	GRADE: ▲
DISTANCE: 26KM	**TOTAL ASCENT:** 993M
START/FINISH: HAYFIELD	**GRID REFERENCE:** 035 869
PARKING: SETT VALLEY TRAIL CAR PARK	**CAFÉ:** GRUMBLEYS BISTRO Tel: 01663 741 444
PUBLIC HOUSE: THE ROYAL HOTEL Tel: 01663 742 721	

WINTER ROUTE TESTING **PHOTO:** GRÁINNE COAKLEY

MAP 19

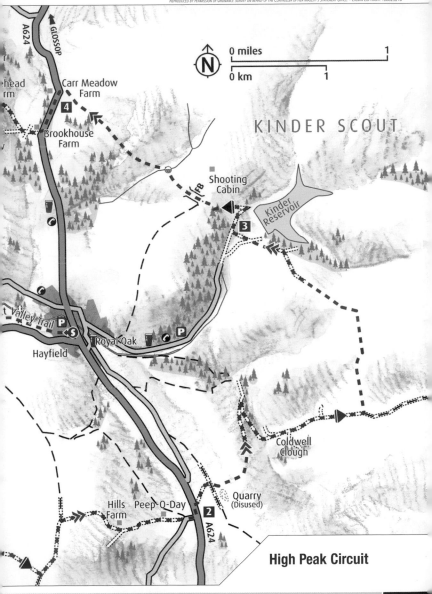

A624

GLOSSOP

head
rm

Carr Meadow
Farm

4

Brookhouse
Farm

KINDER SCOUT

FB

Shooting
Cabin

Kinder
Reservoir

3

Valley Trail

P

S

Royal Oak

P

Hayfield

Coldwell
Clough

Hills
Farm

Peep-O-Day

2

Quarry
(Disused)

A624

0 miles   1

0 km   1

N

High Peak Circuit

Directions – High Peak Circuit

1 Head L out of bottom of **Sett Valley Trail car park**, pass through gate to follow the very flat Sett Valley Trail for approx. 1.5km » After passing large pond continue to junction with road » Turn L uphill to junction with A6015, turn right towards New Mills, take first road L after 250m » Climb tarmac, passing quarries on L » Past Moor Lodge, surface deteriorates – continue uphill ignoring track breaking off L to Piece Farm, track levels to junction » Turn L on bridleway marked by fingerpost » SA uphill through gate – follow bridleway along walled lane, leading out across moors » SA through two gates past steep climb to reach path junction, turn L on bridleway above wall, follow track for 600m to path junction just past gate » SA, (not L and downhill) across moor following RH wall » Join walled lane, continue through several gateways, making steep descent to Hills Farm » **Please walk quietly through garden and shut gate** » Make fast descent on farm track to junction with A624

2 Turn L onto A624, look out for track just before house and barn 100m on R » R up track past old quarry to junction with gravel track, cross track more or less SA to join bridleway (*via Kinder Valley to Edale*) at gate » Follow this track easily up to gate, then descend with interest, bearing L at fork to join tarmac track » R here, cross stream, road curves L up Coldwell Clough » At end of tarmac section take L fork in track. This is the beginning of a tough climb! » Continue SA up track to gate » SA through gate onto hard pack track, up fairly steeply to gate » SA up track across fields to gate » SA through gate, ignore first (locked) gate on L, continue a few metres further uphill, looking out for second gate on L » Through gate, cross moor on indistinct, boggy track, crossing sandy footpath to join wall coming up from L » SA keeping wall on L, look out for gate on L » Through gate, continue on obvious path across fields, pass through open gateway » Descend RW across fields, bear L at stony track beside wood, descend to metal gate » Cross road, SA down steep walled path, turn R to gate leading to walled, cobbled path

3 Through gate then very steeply up walled path, turn sharp L at first junction » Continue steep climb to pass through open gateway, turn L » As track levels out to meet junction continue SA past white shooting cabin on R » Cross wooden footbridge, continue on fabulous singletrack, ford stream, then make fast descent to Glossop Road (A624)

4   Turn L downhill, after 0.6km take R, Lanehead Road on tarmac **»** Descend, then continue steeply uphill on road passing turn off to Blackshaw Farm, then Stet Barn Farm and Lanehead Farm **»** SA where tarmac turns to hard pack, down past Matleymoor Farm **»** R at T-junction along walled track, swinging L and downhill to road (NB. this last section downhill is erroneously marked as a footpath on OS maps) **»** L downhill to house and large gateway, continue SA along walled track (bridleway), ford stream, climb to gate **»** Turn L, descend into Rowarth

5   At village take first L by House (signposted *No Motor Vehicles Except for Access*) **»** Pass telephone box, go through small gate with bridleway fingerpost – head towards white house, passing it on the R – descend track passing more houses to join tarmac **»** L passing front of Little Mill Inn **»** After 430m road forks just before Long Lee, ignore L, continue SA **»** Follow very steep, rocky track uphill **»** Gain flatter section of track **»** Climb again more easily, ignore track coming from L **»** Make fast descent past farm to join road **»** Turn L, after 500m turn R onto bridleway opposite cottages **»** Continue SA at first sharp bend L, descend steep narrow, bumpy path to road **»** Turn L, then L again through gate onto Sett Valley Trail **»** SA back to **Sett Valley Trail car park**

CROSSING THE FOOTBRIDGE ONTO MIDDLE MOOR   PHOTO: ANDY HEADING

KINDER CIRCUIT

GRADE: ▲»▲

DISTANCE: 22KM

TOTAL ASCENT: 946M

START/FINISH: EDALE

GRID REFERENCE: 124 853

PARKING: EDALE CAR PARK

CAFÉ: EDALE COTTAGE CAFÉ (variable opening times) Tel: 01433 670 293

PUBLIC HOUSE: CHESHIRE CHEESE, HOPE. Tel: 01433 620 330.

Kinder Circuit – Kinder

Introduction

This is a superb, ultra-challenging ride with a real 'wilderness feel'. It builds up to a spectacular finale, crossing a 540m high shoulder of Kinder Scout and then descending Jacob's Ladder. Traditionally ridden in the reverse direction, we feel that riding it this way will give the very tough mountain biker the opportunity of staying on his or her bike throughout – in the reverse direction you will be pushing your bike out of Roych Clough and up the Ladder.

Taking in some very spectacular scenery (particularly if there is a dusting of winter snow), via some audacious climbs, this is a real tough cookie that is also furnished with some quality, well scary downhills. Don't underestimate this ride, though it weighs in at a mere 22km, some sections are remote and cover some very demanding terrain – and right near the end it throws in one of the longest climbs in the Peak District!

The Ride

Starting from Edale, a short road climb leads up onto the flanks of Mam Tor. Your first challenge begins here. The single-track climb up to Hollins Cross begins easily enough but soon gets really tough, especially in damp conditions. Stick with it – it is all rideable for the very fit and the very talented! Great singletrack continues up Mam Tor and then down along Cold Side for a quick adrenaline rush; then it's onto Rushop Edge for another big climb and some truly spectacular views as the gradient levels out. The exhilarating descent from here demands respect – then we plummet down on a good track with a rocky drop into Roych Clough. A big 'bread and butter' climb out of the canyon takes us up for some more good quality single-track before cutting around the side of Mount Famine *via* another short climb and an exciting descent. Then comes the big one – 300m of ascent, gruelling at first, easing slightly in the middle then rocky and technical at the end. You will be well rewarded at the top, because the descent of Jacob's Ladder is a real plum prize – especially if taken on a quiet day when there aren't too many walkers on the trail. From here you'll be buzzing all the way on a pleasant cruise back to the car park.

KINDER

Kinder Low

Wool Pac

Swine's
Back

4

Jacob's La

Edale
Cross

3

Coldwell
Clough

P

HAYFIELD

Mount
Famine

HIGH PEAK

The
Roych

Roych Clough

A624

A6

STOCKPORT

New
Smithy

Breckend

Chapel
Milton

A6(T)

MAP 20

Kinder Circuit

Directions – Kinder Circuit

1   R out of **Edale car park** towards Barber Booth » Pass works entrance then 1st L down metalled track, cross stream then steadily uphill past Hardenclough Farm » Bear L, cross stream, continue steeply up to gate on L (just before Greenlands) » Through gate, L up pleasant gravel singletrack » Climb continues with increasing difficulty up through two gates then into particularly challenging section up to cross roads » At viewpoint, Hollins Cross – take right path up flagstones and through gate » Continue climb upward, bear right towards shoulder, joining short but exhilarating singletrack descent to gate » Through gate and steeply L up road » Descend very slightly, look out for gate on R » Through gate then begin climb up Rushop Edge » Continue climb through gate, continue SA along vague level track, below ridge, look for small gate on R, just after larger gate » Open gate using unusual latch, descend L to fork in path by gate » SA through gate then either follow precarious singletrack on L or straight down rocky sunken section » At bottom follow path adjacent to road, then bear right at gate to join track that eventually descends into Roych Clough

2   Drop down steadily to cross stream then SA through gate » continue SA, cross stream to gate, through this into walled track that culminates in rock steps dropping down to ford at base of Roych Clough » Steeply out of clough, continue up track to gate » SA at gate, continue to climb less steeply, ignore BW branching off L » SA up track, now more steeply up to small col » Continue on good track for fast flowing descent to gate » SA then bear right down to gate and into walled hard pack track » SA smoothly downhill for 400m – look for track on R, just before farm shacks (signposted *Via Kinder Valley to Edale*) » Follow this track easily up to gate, then descend with interest, bearing L at fork to join metalled track » R here, cross steam, road curves L up Coldwell Clough » At end of tarmac section take L fork in track (more or less SA) » Up this is the beginning of a very tough climb!

3 SA through gate onto hard pack track, up fairly steeply to gate » SA up track across fields to gate (signed *Edale*) » SA up track, steady at first, then increasingly steep and rocky – continue for 1.4km with great determination to gate at Edale Cross » Past here track eventually flattens slightly before short sharp climb takes you to beginning of descent proper

4 Jacob's Ladder – classic descent begins with tricky section on steep steps » Continue with slightly less difficulty then take sharp R to gate (ignore FP on L) » SA on easier terrain before dropping steeply L into loose, stony walled track with gate at bottom » Through gate, cross footbridge, through gate » Follow track SA for 1.8km through several gates to Upper Booth » SA along tarmac road which curves sharp L, eventually passing parking spot and dropping beneath railway viaduct into Barber Booth » L along road to **Edale car park**

PHOTO: ANDY HEADING

PHOTO: *ANDY HEADING*

Mam Tor Classic – Hope Valley

Introduction

A superb excursion that makes the most of the riding across a complex of high ridges between Castleton and Ladybower. Avoiding any overly technical climbs, this should be a fairly evenly paced ride, fully rideable even on first acquaintance – just keep focussed on the loose steep ascent out of Jaggers Clough. We've included a couple of options here which will allow you to customise the ride for future variety.

The Ride

From the busy little tourist honeypot of Castleton, this route takes us up via an extraordinary crumpled sheet of collapsed tarmac and some easy road work onto a high pass. Leaving this, it's up again, this time via some great quality singletrack, out onto the spectacular summit ridge of Mam Tor; then down *via* a mouth-watering choice of thrilling descents! From Edale (optional brew stop) there's an easily won climb before the steep descent into and ascent out of Jaggers Clough. Near the top, the route joins an old Roman road, contouring round through some fine scenery to a superb, stony descent. After crossing the frantic A57 Snake Pass, there is another steep uphill, this time mainly on a good tarmac surface, joining another quality summit ridge which takes us to Crook Hill and two options for descent. From here it's a cruise on back roads to the starting point.

MAM TOR CLASSIC
GRADE: ▲ » ▲

DISTANCE: 24KM Plus any optional extensions
START/FINISH: CASTLETON
PARKING: CASTLETON CAR PARK
CAFÉ: COTTAGE CAFÉ (variable opening times) Tel: 01433 670 293
PUBLIC HOUSE: THE PEAKS INN, CASTLETON Tel: 01433 620 247

TOTAL ASCENT: 1136M
GRID REFERENCE: 150 830

PHOTO: ANDY HEADING

PHOTO: ANDY HEADING

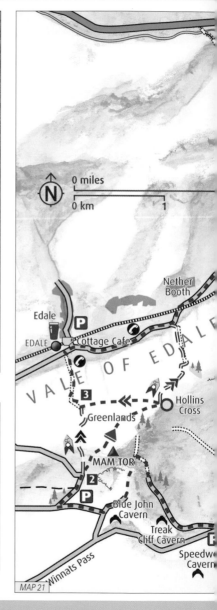

N

0 miles 1
0 km 1

Nether Booth

Edale

EDALE
P
Cottage Cafe

VALE OF EDALE

3
Greenlands

Hollins Cross

MAM TOR

2
P

Blue John Cavern

Treak Cliff Cavern

Speedwell Cavern

Winnats Pass

MAP 21

Directions – Mam Tor Classic

1 Follow A6187 west out of **Castleton** » Straight on along old road past Treak Cliff Cavern » Continue SA past bus turning area and up on steep tarmac through gate » Continue up collapsing tarmac road to gate at top – watch out for drop offs! » Continue along short stretch of road to join main road, turn R » Follow main road for 0.5km, turn R steeply uphill just past parking area » Follow road up then descend slightly – look for gate on R by bus stop » Through gate, either straight ahead or drop down left for:

Option A:
Good, steep descent – handle with care. Bear L down stony shoot to gate » Through gate into steep, rutted descent, eventually leading to another gate » Join road by Greenlands – junction with Option B (*below*)

2 Continue SA on good singletrack » Over shoulder into descent to gate, once through gate continue SA on stone flags through second gate to four-way path junction (Hollins Cross) » Drop L, bear L again (Option B) or right (Option C)

Option B:
Good quality descent. Bear L, tricky at first with a few drop offs » Continue SA, fast, rutted and absorbing to gate » SA through second gate, continue along smoother track to junction with Option A (*above*) by Greenlands

Option C:

Another great descent. Bear R, below Hollins Cross, weave down on exciting and technical singletrack. Though less sustained than Options A or B, this descent throws in some very tricky obstacles – especially in slippery conditions.

3 For **Options A & B**: Turn R out of gate near Greenlands, descending steeply on tarmac to road, turn R **»** Continue SA along road, passing under railway bridge just past **junction with Option C**. After youth hostel and riding school, look out for gate on L – bridleway entrance (signed *Footpath and Bridleway to Alport*) **»** Through gate, SA up walled path, cross ford, through gate **»** SA up pleasant track through two gates **»** At second gate, SA for steep descent into Jaggers Clough – get into low gear before ford and gate **»** Cross ford, through gate, SA up steep, loose track **»** Track eases somewhat up to gate, through gate, SA to junction with Roman road.

4 L here up stony track, SA to gate **»** SA, cross stream at Blackley Clough, through awkward gate – after slight rise track descends **»** Great descent, very loose and stony to join tarmac **»** R through gate, steep descent on tarmac to cross stream, then up steeply to A57 Snake Pass **»** Cross busy and dangerous A57 **with care**, SA up farm track **»** Continue through gate past Rowlee Farm, zig-zag up steep tarmac/gravel road which flattens off before reaching gate **»** SA through gate, continue up to second gate, through this to meet cross roads **»** Bear R on singletracks keeping woods to your L, picking up main track. Do not descend on track or continue on main track signed *Fairholmes, past Lockerbrook*.

5 Continue SA with woods on L, good singletrack options across fairly flat ground to gate **»** Through gate, continue SA as track becomes steeper to double gates **»** SA through gate, cross moorland (usually boggy), joining more definite path as it descends to gate, through gate, choice of two options:

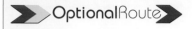

Option D:
This shorter option is better during the wet winter months or if you're struggling for time: » SA across field, bearing L round the peculiar formation of Crook Hill, joining more definite track down through Crookhill Farm and onto steep tarmac track » Join road at bottom of track, go R to junction with busy A57 » L here, onto cycle path, follow this to lights » R at lights, continue along cycle path next to A6103 to dam » Cross dam to junction with Option E

Option E:
The longer option adds useful mileage for the summer months: » R through gate, descend slightly to second gate, wall on R » Descend SA down grassy track through field to join track coming from L at gate » R through gate and into woods, fast descent, often slippery to join A57 at bottom » Cross road **with care**, head R along A57 » After 0.5km, take first L down gravel track, cross bridge to head L along S bank of Ladybower Reservoir » Easily R along track for 5km, finishing with easy climb up hard pack before track curves R and then descends to dam, junction with (Option D)

6 From dam continue down track (tarmac at first), looking out for permitted bridleway after 0.25km on R » Continue SA through two gates to meet road, head R uphill » On reaching village of Thornhill, take R turn just before telephone box – Carr Lane (signposted *Not Suitable for Motors*) » Steadily uphill to Aston » SA through village, follow road as it bears L then descends steeply to drop beneath railway bridge to join A6187 – turn R crossing river into Hope » Turn L just before church, L at T-junction, cross stream and head uphill to pass Hope Valley Cement Works on L » Continue steadily uphill on quiet road before descending SA into **Castleton** at acute fork » Into village and back to the car/pub

RICHARD MANTERFIELD DESCENDING MAM TOR **PHOTO:** *ANDY HEADING*

Stanage – East Peak

Introduction

This is a route following trails that have become firm favourites with many Sheffield locals, easily linked into the city via the **Sheffield City Links** at points (2 & 3) – this linkup makes a superb and challenging day ride.

Describing a lazy figure of eight, this circuit incorporates a fair amount of road-work, especially at the beginning, but the views are good and the rewards are great as downhill action is fully maximised and the best riding is left 'til last.

The Ride

Leaving the pay and display car park below Stanage Edge, height is gained easily on tarmac through some picturesque terrain. Keep pedalling and enjoy the views as you swing by the Burbage Valley, drop slightly to Ringinglow and then cut out across Houndkirk Moor. A swift and exhilarating descent then brings you down for another brief section on tarmac before plummeting into Blacka Plantation on one of the Peaks tighter bits of steep and technical single-track. Climbing up from here, the route then joins up with the classic crossing of Houndkirk Moor before another leisurely road section weaves round to Redmires. Here you leave the road and climb with increasing interest up to Stanage Pole. Pause a while – it's a great situation. As we said, the best is definitely saved for last as a choice of two contrasting but equally great downhills will take you back more or less directly to the car park.

STANAGE	GRADE: ▲

DISTANCE: 24KM (OPTION A) 27.5KM (OPTION B) **TOTAL ASCENT:** 688M
START/FINISH: STANAGE PLANTATION   **GRID REFERENCE:** 238 838
PARKING: STANAGE PLANTATION PAY AND DISPLAY CAR PARK
CAFÉ: OUTSIDE CAFÉ Tel: 01433 651 936
PUBLIC HOUSE: THE NORFOLK ARMS, RINGINGLOW Tel: 0114 230 2197

PHOTO: ANDY HEADING

MAP 22

Stanage

Directions – Stanage

1   L out of **Stanage Plantation car park »** Continue along road below Stanage Edge, bear L at junction with road coming up from R **»** Continue SA, L at Junction with road coming up from R, continue uphill for 1.6km to next junction, bear L **»** Follow road as it curves R around parking spot overlooking Burbage Valley (Fiddlers Elbow) **»** Continue SA for another 2.5km – look out for gate next to woods on R which leads onto track across moor **•** Cross road to gate, Continue SA through gate across moor, trees on L **»** Track climbs slightly before descending with interest to four way junction – straight across into fast descent to gate **•** Through gate, R along Sheephill Road

2   Continue along Sheephill Road which descends slightly to junction **»** R at junction, uphill for 0.6km, look out for bridleway on L (signposted *Bridleway to Shorts Lane*), leading down through gap in wall and into trees – start of good descent **»** Make descent (steep, narrow and technical) to cross wooden bridge and meet wider path at bottom **»** L down this path then SA to ford on R (SA for **Sheffield City Link – Return** *see page 184*) **»** Turn R, cross ford and begin challenging climb **»** Climb continues up steps, then steepens to junction near bench – head R and up, eventually meeting gate **»** SA through gate, cross fields bearing R to join track that leads to A625 **»** Turn L at road (which becomes A6187), SA past L turn to wide track on R **»** Head along track to gate on R **»** Head though gate and along byway **»** Track climbs then continues to undulate for 2.5km to four-way junction passed through earlier, continue SA past two gates to join Sheephill Road

3   Turn L onto Sheephill Road, continue to stepped junction next to old Toll House, turn L **»** Turn R to join Fulwood Lane – SA for 1km, road dips slightly then rises past junction with Greenhouse Lane (junction with **Sheffield City Link – Out** *see page 180*) **»** Continue SA along Fulwood Lane for 2.8km **»** Road drops steeply to junction at bottom – turn L, continue SA, follow road as it curves R **»** Turn L at junction, drop down into dip past entrance to Wyming Brook **»** SA up hill, continue past water works on L – road curves L past Redmires Reservoir **»** At end of road, bear R and up to begin interesting climb to gate **»** SA through gate, up to Stanage Pole, bear R from here on rough track for approx. 600m – from here there are two options for descent:

>OptionalRoute>

Option A:
Keep a close look out for blue bridleway markers pointing L off track **»** Cross moor onto top of Stanage Edge, bear R for a few metres looking for stone flagged path leading down L – you need to cross a rock ledge and drop in somewhat to reach it – handle with care! **»** Continue down flags with great interest to pass through gate **»** Continue downhill to next gate, through gate **»** **Do not bear R to car park**, head L after a few metres down fast, indistinct path– watch out for ditch before the road **»** Turn R at road then R into **Stanage Plantation car park**

>OptionalRoute>

Option B:
From Stanage Pole bear R, continue to bear R following increasingly rough track down the causeway **»** Bear L through rocky section into loose stuff which eventually becomes faster and a little smoother as you bear L to parking spot and junction with road **»** L at road, coast down then slightly up to reach **Stanage Plantation car park** on L

PHOTO: ANDY HEADING

TOP TEN HILL CLIMBS IN THE DARK PEAK

There are many killer climbs in the Dark Peak. Here are a few to test the mettle – even of the most dedicated specialist. Only one rule that needs to be obeyed to make a claim – no foot-downs allowed.

1   **Jacobs Ladder** The mother of all climbs – included here more as a challenge to the mighty than anything else. The first section is loose and steep and has most folks off their bikes before the corner. The middle section relents somewhat and though rutted and tricky is ride-able by most mortals. The last section past the rock steps could well be the hardest section of technical climbing in the Dark Peak - is this the ultimate test?

2   **Edale to Hollins Cross** The first climb on our mega-challenging Kinder Circuit – now confirmed as do-able by a member of our proofing team! A good effort will almost certainly guarantee applause from the weekend gatherings at Hollins Cross.

3   **Gores Heights** OK it looks fine on first acquaintance, but in the winter months this dark and dank uphill is slippery and often coated with decaying leaves. At any time of year the awkward rock steps appear at just the wrong time for a clean ascent. A formidable challenge.

4   **Swallows Pride** This is the return climb up the black route from the first descent on our Wharncliffe Cross Country circuit. The first section of uphill gives a steady taster of what's to come – then the climb mellows off for a while. The sting in the tail is the rocky section at the top, where full determination is required for success.

check out
www.v-graphics.co.uk
for detailed information
& co-ordinates

5 Stanage Causeway The roman road that makes a long elegant curve up onto Stanage Edge is a classic off road climb. Never overly steep, the surface makes up for this by contriving to stay very loose and chucking in an endless series of tricky steps that always seem to be out of line!

6 Chinley Churn – On the ascent to New Allotments – last 500m
Definitely do-able - in the dry, if you're feeling strong! Hyper-ventilation guaranteed.

7 Rushop Edge A challenging climb in a perfect situation. If you can master the start out of the gate at the bottom (often very slippery, but OK in dry conditions), there's no reason that you'll not make it to the top without a foot-down. It's difficult to avoid being distracted by the superb views.

8 Jaggers Clough Starting from the gate in the ford at the bottom of Jaggers Clough is just the start of this challenging climb. Wet wheels do not help on the loose gravel steepness and it's essential to keep your front wheel down to avoid impersonating the Lone Ranger. Quite a short-lived climb but satisfying once mastered – the question is can you do it every time?

9 Win Hill from Aston From the tiny village of Aston, there's a steep farm track that helps establish a good burn early on. From the top of this you enter a walled track that is usually damp with a muddy, loose surface – tricky to master on first acquaintance. If you make it to the top of this track you can relax as open singletrack rolls out across the side of Win Hill where the contours are easily gained right to the top.

10 Porter Clough OK, not a desperate climb but loose and steep and a classic rite-of-passage that, once conquered, will live on in the heart of any Sheffield based mountain biker. Your first proper technical climb?

Killer Loops
sponsored by

SECTION **4**

Killer Loops

Killer Loops

Weighing in or around the sturdy 50km mark – meaning that plenty of character building experience will be required to complete a killer loop. Owing to the uncompromising nature of the climbing, even the experienced enduro veteran will find these challenging – allow plenty of time, stock up well on the calories and make sure you're firing on all four cylinders.

BIG RING TERRITORY **PHOTO**: JOHN HOULIHAN

Bleaklow Circuit – Upper Derwent

Introduction

Pedalling in a big loop around Bleaklow, this is the mother of all classics and an essential rite-of-passage for any Peak District mountain biker. Though there are a lot of road miles, this route definitely shouldn't be underestimated – it's long, tough and tiring.

We recommend that you undertake it during the longer days of summer and set out properly equipped.

The Ride

We have chosen to describe the route from a start at Fairholmes pay and display car park; there are other potential starting points for this route.

After scooting down on easy roads along the eastern bank of Ladybower, we make a steep ascent that begins on tarmac and brings us up onto Crook Hill. Some quality singletrack along this ridge leads to a fast descent past Rowlee Farm. Here we join the Snake Pass for some serious bread and butter road kilometres. Leaving The Snake, it's off out into the wilderness *via* the course of a Roman road before tackling the truly wild and potentially dangerous plummet down Doctor's Gate.

Skirting round Glossop, we then join the picturesque and easy going Longdendale Trail for some more easily won kilometres. The going toughens somewhat towards the end as we cross the Woodhead Pass, initially up *via* some gravely switchbacks, more tarmac and then down via the bleak and rutted Snow Road to rejoin the Woodhead Road.

Finally it's off again into the wilderness. This time for a real treat, the remote and challenging Cut Gate Path across the bleak Howden Moors. A super-classic singletrack descent from here, and some easy hard pack tracks along the picturesque eastern bank of Howden and Derwent Reservoirs constitute a fitting finale.

BLEAKLOW CIRCUIT   GRADE: ▲

DISTANCE: 62KM
START/FINISH: FAIRHOLMES
PARKING: FAIRHOLMES CAR PARK
PUBLIC HOUSE: THE SNAKE PASS INN Tel: 01433 651 480

TOTAL ASCENT: 2387M
GRID REFERENCE: 173 894
CAFÉ: FAIRHOLMES VISITORS CENTRE Tel: 01433 650 953

MAP 23

Trans-Pennine Trail

Snow Road

SHEFFIELD ➤

7

8

Langsett Reservoir

nead Reservoir

HOWDEN MOORS

AKLOW

Gut Gate

9

4

A57 Snake Pass

0 miles 1

0 km 1

N

Snake Pass Inn

Rowlee Farm

DERWENT MOORS

Derwent Reservoir

S

Fairholmes

3

ER UT

Ladybower Reservoir

2

SHEFFIELD ➤

Crookhill Farm

A57

Edale
EDALE

LOSE HILL

Bleaklow Circuit

Directions – Bleaklow Circuit

1 Head R out of **Fairholmes car park**, impressive dam wall of Derwent Reservoir should be on your L, road curves round up R passing Jubilee Cottages and telephone box » About 4km of tarmac and hard pack leads across Mill Brook to join A57 » Turn R across viaduct then R again up road on W bank of reservoir, look out for very steep tarmac road on L after 0.6km » Follow bridleway markers up and through Crookhill Farm, bearing right through two gates to join track up onto Crook Hill

2 Follow RH wall, ignore all tracks that fork L » Through gate, follow wall for approx. 100m then bear L to cross exposed moorland – follow wooden marker posts towards gate » SA through gate and up through field (signposted *Bridleway to Rowlee Farm and Lockerbrook*) to gate » SA through gate, easy riding following wooden stakes to another gate » SA through gate, fast descent with woods on R to double gates » Ignore bridleway leading R, SA through gates » Follow interesting sand and gravel track for 1km to gate and junction with larger track » Follow track uphill to junction with good track » L on good gravel farm track, leading down to steep, fast section with tight bends and then through gate past farm, **carefully join Snake Pass** (A57)

3 At bottom of farm track turn R onto busy and dangerous A57 » Follow A57 for 8km, passing the Snake Inn after 4.75km – look out for lay by and National Trust sign on RH side of road, 1km after emerging from woodland

4 From lay by on R (signposted *Doctor's Gate*), SA through gate, follow track to cross ford » SA along paving flag track to four way cross roads » SA to descend very rough track (Roman road), very technical at first, keep river on R » SA down track which eases slightly but continues to throw in some very difficult sections » After approx. 3km from cross roads, and after crossing river twice, join smooth fast track to gate » Through gate, take RH bridge (ignore L which leads to farm)

5 After 2.3km and another gate, track turns into Shepley Street, passing works on R » Turn R at T-junction then SA passing church on L, L along Wellgate/Church Street to fork » Follow R fork to join Woodhead Road » R along Woodhead Road for 0.5km to L turn into Cemetery Road, continue past staggered junction, descend to Padfield Railway Station along Park Road » Bear R, then R again into car park and entrance to Longdendale Trail » SA along flat, well graded trail for 7km, crossing B6105 at approx. half way

6 At end of trail turn L, cross dam (Woodhead Reservoir) to join the very busy Woodhead Road (A628), turn R » Continue SA along A628 for 1.75km, past point at which A6024 forks off L, cross Woodhead Bridge, looking out for L turn up track » Turn L, ignore steep concrete path leading L uphill – go through gate next to small stone barn » SA up walled track, steady climb onto Pikenaze Moor, pass through gate onto undulating track, eventually to join A628

7 **Cross A628 with care**, pass through small gap in crash barriers opposite » Descend grass track to cross narrow stone bridge over Salter's Brook, climb SA up steep grass track » Continue along track which curves L (N) across moor to meet A628 opposite road junction » R along road for 2.16km, look out for marked bridleway – Snow Road – leaving road at acute angle on L, pass through wooden 5-bar gate » SA along rutted track, mainly in descent to join A628 » L along A628 for 0.5km until just past Milton Lodge – look out for waymarked bridleway beside Bord Hill Farm » Cross road and through metal 5-bar gate, descend slightly for 200m to sharp LH turn onto Swinden Lane – through the upper of two LH gates

8 Follow walled lane slightly downhill through three gateways » At fourth take L turn down farm track to fork » Take L fork on grassier track into Crookland Wood » Turn R after 400m – SA down steep track to cross Brook House Bridge » SA up gravel track which curves R, becoming quite steep and rocky » Continue up path onto open moorland, continue SA past steps » Ignore path veering L – continue SA past short descent to Haslingshaw Stream, begin long climb up LH side of Mickledon Beck » Continue SA, steadily uphill along Mickledon Edge (Cut Gate), ignore L turn and fingerpost – rideable pretty well all of the way with determination and in good conditions ('cos you're still fresh, right?) » Path joins stream bed – continue SA through tougher terrain, continuing SA until ground levels out

9 From large cairn at Howden Edge, begin great descent, first peaty and rutted, then onto fast flags, into dirt singletrack, into loose & stony path, finally dropping into Cranberry Clough » Look out for, and take singletrack contouring off L before first steps and then **look out for and follow blue bridleway marker pointing L** » After steep drop into clough, follow side of stream to join track coming from R » L along track continue SA as it rises above river, ignoring turn to old pack horse bridge at Slippery Stones on R » SA along track – it levels out then descends to join E bank of Howden Reservoir, continuing on to join tarmac by Jubilee Cottages and phone box » Turn sharp R down tarmac, descend with dam wall on R, turn L into **Fairholmes car park** – you've made it back!

Killer Loop – Hope Valley

Introduction

Obviously, there are a multitude of options for linking together sections of riding from the routes in this book.

This is one option – a very challenging route, which we hope will be looked back on as a tough, thoroughly satisfying, balanced day out with the emphasis very much on downhill fun (some of the best downhills in the Peak are included here for your enjoyment).

Though there are some tough climbs, most of these are kept on tarmac and, apart from the gruelling slog up past Gores Heights, the fit mountain biker may have a good chance of 'styling' this demanding route.

The Ride

Very long and very tough!

KILLER LOOP   GRADE: ▲

DISTANCE: 57KM   **TOTAL ASCENT:** 2354M
START/FINISH: CASTLETON   **GRID REFERENCE:** 149 830
PARKING: CASTLETON PAY AND DISPLAY CAR PARK **CAFÉ:** WOODBINE CAFÉ, HOPE Tel: 01433 621 407
PUBLIC HOUSE: LOTS TO CHOOSE FROM IN CASTLETON

continues on
NEXT PAGE

Nether
Booth

Edale
EDALE

P

LOSE HILL

Hardenclough
Farm

Hollins
Cross

3

Greenlands

Rushop Edge

MAM TOR

P

Blue John
Cavern

Treak
Cliff Cavern

P **S**

2

Castleton

Cavedale

Speedwell
Cavern

Peak
Cavern

Pin Dale

quarry

Eldon Hill

Quarrys

N 0 miles 1

0 km 1

MAP 24

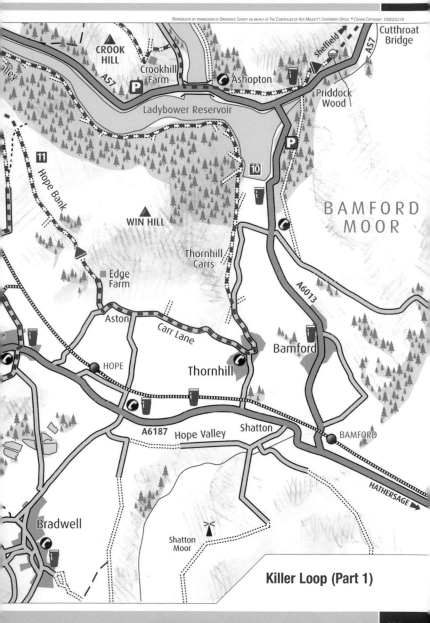

Cutthroat
Bridge

CROOK
HILL

Sheffield

Crookhill
Farm

Ashopton

A57

Priddock
Wood

Ladybower Reservoir

11

10

Hope Bank

BAMFORD
MOOR

WIN HILL

Thornhill
Carrs

Edge
Farm

A6013

Aston

Carr Lane

Bamford

HOPE

Thornhill

A6187

Hope Valley

Shatton

BAMFORD

Bradwell

HATHERSAGE

Shatton
Moor

Killer Loop (Part 1)

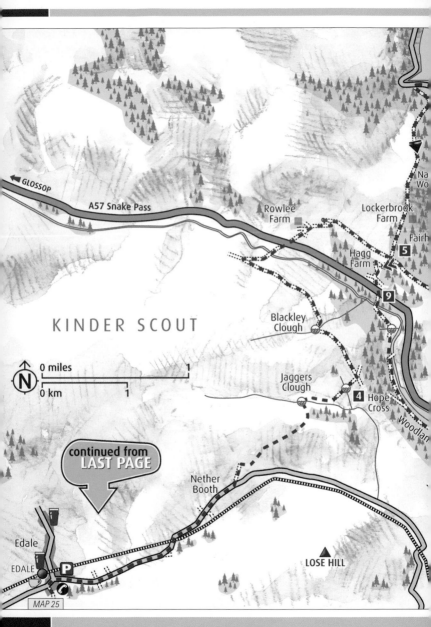

← GLOSSOP

A57 Snake Pass

Rowlee
Farm

Lockerbrook
Farm

Na
Wo

Fairh

5

Hagg
Farm

9

KINDER SCOUT

Blackley
Clough

Jaggers
Clough

4 Hope
Cross

Woodlan

N
0 miles   1
0 km   1

continued from
LAST PAGE

Nether
Booth

Edale

EDALE

P

MAP 25

LOSE HILL

Killer Loop (Part 2)

Directions – Killer Loop

1 L out of car park take first R into *Castle Street* bear L, head uphill **»** Where road splits at acute angle, take R steeply uphill **»** Follow road past LH turn off into Pin Dale, turn R onto Dirtlow Rake track **»** Follow track parallel to road then up and away from road **»** SA along track past large quarry on R **»** SA through gate **»** At bridleway crossroads, take track through gate on R **»** Follow track across field signposted *Castleton*, bearing down and slightly R towards small gate in drystone wall (**ignore 4WD tracks leading off up and SA**) **»** Through gate, follow track down and L into Cavedale, keeping wall on L to gate **»** Through gate, track becomes very steep and very rocky (full on trials skills required for success!), eventually easing as dale opens out, continue SA to gate

2 SA Through gate, turn L dropping down through village to main road, A6187, west out of Castleton **»** Follow this SA along old road past Treak Cliff Cavern **»** Continue SA past bus turning area and up on steep tarmac through gate **»** Continue up collapsing tarmac road to gate at top – watch out for drop offs! **»** Continue along short stretch of road to join main road, turn R **»** Follow road for 0.5km, turn R steeply uphill just past parking area **»** Follow road up then descend slightly – look for gate on R by bus stop **»** Through gate, continue SA on good singletrack **»** Continue over shoulder into descent to gate, once through gate continue SA on stone flags through second gate to four-way path junction (Hollins Cross)

3 Drop L, bear L again for good quality descent – this is tricky at first with a few drop offs **»** Continue SA, fast, rutted and absorbing to gate **»** SA through second gate, continue along smoother track to gate by Greenlands **»** R out of gate, descend steeply on tarmac to join road – turn R **»** Continue SA along road, passing under railway bridge – look out for gate on L just after riding school – bridleway entrance signed *Alport* **»** Through gate, SA up walled path, cross ford, through gate **»** SA up pleasant track, through two gates **»** At second gate continue SA for steep descent into Jaggers Clough – get into low gear before ford and gate **»** Cross ford, through gate, SA up steep, loose track **»** Track eases somewhat up to gate, through gate, SA to junction with Roman road at Hope Cross

4   L here up stony track, SA to gate **»** SA, cross stream at Blackley Clough, through awkward gate – after slight rise track descends **»** Great descent, very loose and stony to join tarmac **»** R through gate, steep descent on tarmac to cross stream, then up steeply to A57 Snake Pass **» Cross busy A57 with care**, SA up farm track **»** Continue through gate past Rowlee Farm, zig zag up steep tarmac/gravel road which flattens off before reaching gate **»** SA through gate, continue up to second gate, through this to meet cross roads **»** Bear right on singletracks keeping woods to your left to pick up larger track, **do not descend on wide track or continue on main track**

5   Continue SA with woods on L, good singletrack options across fairly flat ground to gate **»** Through gate, continue SA as track becomes steeper to double gates **»** SA through gates, cross moorland (usually boggy), joining more definite path as it descends to gate, through gate **»** SA across field, bearing L round the peculiar formation of Crook Hill, joining more definite track down through Crookhill Farm and onto steep tarmac track **»** Join road at bottom of track, go R to junction with busy A57

6   Turn l, cross bridge, take first L up track, looking out for white gate on R **»** Head R through gate past houses – head uphill on increasingly gravelly surface, through second gate **»** Follow track upwards, then down next to wall to meet T-junction with track coming up through gate on R **»** SA past gate, head up on tricky surface until fork in track – continue SA **»** Cross moor, trees on R, to stream crossing – cross stream, through gate **»** Cross moor on good track to fork, take L fork **»** Descend slightly as track curves L above Cutthroat Bridge

7   Take L fork up for brilliant singletrack ascent **»** After 1.5km join crossroads (good views from small bluff on L) **»** SA (marked bridleway) to good, testing singletrack below Whinstone Lee Tor – wall on L **»** Look out for L turn through gate to begin superb, rolling descent **»** Through gate, follow singletrack with wall on L **»** Through gate into steep rocky section, cross ford, through large gate to enter courtyard between two ancient barns – look for small gate on L **»** Drop down steep flagstones, bearing R to gate, straight on here on hard track **»** Along E edge of Ladybower Reservoir, curve L and cross Mill Brook, soon reaching tarmac road **»** About 1.5km along this look out for telephone box and Jubilee Cottages **»** Just past this point follow tarmac road (not track), curving down L below wall of Derwent Dam to reach Fairholmes.

8 **Alternative Fairholmes start.** From Fairholmes turn right at mini roundabout, head through gates » Continue along W side of Ladybower on tarmac for 1.9km » After Gores Farm, curve L round corner – look out for gate and track leading up sharp L into trees » Continue up track which becomes very steep and slippery in all but the driest of conditions – a notable climb! » Continue up lessening steepness, descend slightly past Lockerbrook Farm » Cross stream and go SA through gate – easy climb for short distance up wider track » 0.4km after farm, track forks » Drop L, through gate, into superb descent with bermed corners » Through gate superb descent continues with loose and rocky sections, soon joining hard pack – drop steeply and with care to A57

9 **Cross busy A57 with care** » Through gate, down steep and often slippery descent » Curve R, cross bridge, continue L and then up track – often very muddy » Track forks at gate, L through gate and descend to S bank of Ladybower Reservoir » Easily along track for 5km, finishing with easy climb up hard pack before track curves R and then descends to dam

10 Instead of crossing dam, continue down track, looking out for permitted bridleway after 0.25km on R » Continue SA through two gates to meet road, head R uphill » On reaching village of Thornhill, take R turn just before telephone box – Carr Lane (signposted *Not Suitable for Motors*) » Steadily uphill to Aston, through village, look out for R turn uphill on tarmac (signposted *Win Hill and Hope Cross*) » Continue uphill, turning L at Edge farm to join muddy walled bridleway » Track levels off slightly, undulating beneath the SW flank of Win Hill » At junction with wide bridleway, descend L to join wide sandy track (Roman road)

11 Descend 0.5km then take an acute L on wide track just before gate (almost doubling back) for long, fast swoop down the flank of Win Hill – not without interest and mainly in descent – eventually joining farmtrack at gate » Roll down track bearing R onto road » Bear L along road, under bridge into Hope » Turn L just before church, L at T-junction, cross stream and head uphill to pass Hope Valley Cement Works on L » Continue steadily uphill on quiet road before descending SA into **Castleton** at acute fork » Into village and back to the car/pub

Lord of the Loops – The Peak District

Introduction

Come and have a go if you think you're hard enough!

The Lord of the Loops is designed for the athletic rider who has done everything and is seeking the next big challenge.

The Ride

The Lord of the Loops is big! Covering over 100km of gruellingly hilly terrain, an early start should be deemed essential – and unless you're well fit already, you will need to train!

Owing to limitations of space, we've supplied you with a sketch map for guidance only – full details of the route are available from the **'Mountain Biking in the Dark Peak CD'** *(see page 190)*.

LORD OF THE LOOPS   GRADE: ▲▲

DISTANCE: 105KM+

START/FINISH: LADYBOWER RESERVOIR

PARKING: FAIRHOLMES CAR PARK

CAFÉ: FAIRHOLMES, CASTLETON AND HAYFIELD

TOTAL ASCENT: 4022M

GRID REFERENCE: 173 894

PUBLIC HOUSE: WAIT 'TIL THE END! – LADYBOWER INN Tel: 01433 651 241

PHOTO: *ANDY HEADING*

PHOTO: *ANDY HEADING*

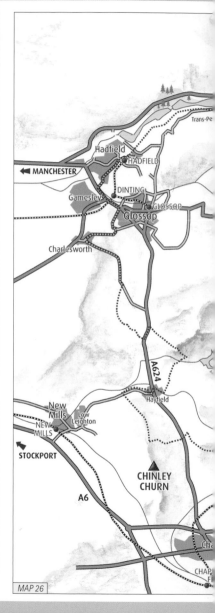
MAP 26

The Lord of the Loops

A to B Rides
sponsored by

www.lumicycle.co.uk

SECTION 5

A to B Rides

TYPICAL CHALLENGING DARK PEAK DESCENT **PHOTO:** ANDY HEADING

A to B Rides

Two challenging rides that start out in The Peak and end up back in the city. Use the train or get dropped off – the choice is up to you. Either way there is something of a psychological advantage that comes with the knowledge that each pedal stroke is bringing you closer to home, the shower and a nice cup of tea.

Edale to New Mills – West Peak

Introduction

A direct route across the highest pass in Middle England, this ancient route is now accessible using modern mountain biking technology. Although relatively short and very direct, it is a challenging ride in the mountains.

The Ride

Leaving the isolated hamlet of Edale, a pleasant warm up leads to a hefty push up to Edale Cross. This sets you up for the superb, fast descent into Coldwell Clough on the edge of Hayfield. Hard climbing then carries you over Chinley Churn, before more excellent riding lands you into New Mills. This is the most direct route, but armed with an OS map, there are many, many variations, extensions and, of course, return loops. The most obvious is to continue down the Goyt Way and catch the train home from Marple.

EDALE TO NEW MILLS	GRADE: ▲»▲
DISTANCE: 15.5KM	**TOTAL ASCENT:** 687M
START: EDALE	**GRID REFERENCE:** 124 853
FINISH: NEW MILLS CENTRAL STATION	**GRID REFERENCE:** 998 854
PARKING: ARRIVE BY TRAIN!	**CAFÉ:** COTTAGE CAFÉ Tel: 01433 670 293
PUBLIC HOUSE: THE RAMBLER Tel: 01433 670 268	

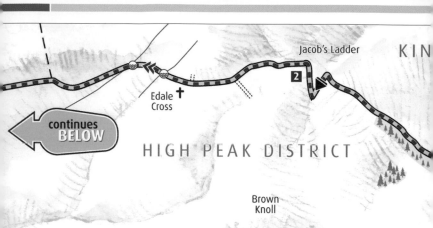

Jacob's Ladder

KIN

Edale
Cross

continues
BELOW

HIGH PEAK DISTRICT

Brown
Knoll

0 miles 1

0 km 1

N

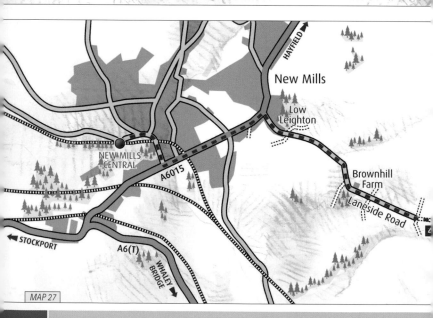

HAYFIELD

New Mills

Low
Leighton

NEW MILLS
CENTRAL

A6015

Brownhill
Farm

Laneside Road

STOCKPORT

A6(T)

WHALEY
BRIDGE

MAP 27

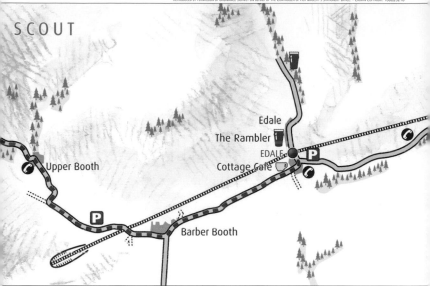

SCOUT

Edale

The Rambler

EDALE

Upper Booth

Cottage Cafe

P

Barber Booth

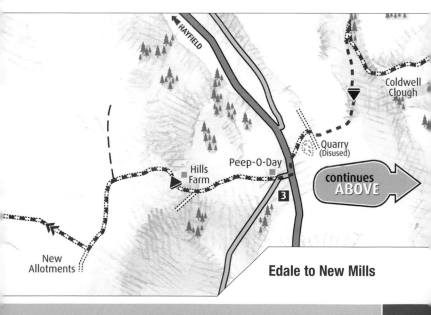

HAYFIELD

Coldwell
Clough

Quarry
(Disused)

Peep-O-Day

Hills
Farm

3

**continues
ABOVE**

New
Allotments

Edale to New Mills

Directions – Edale to New Mills

1 R out of **Edale station**, then R and along lane, turning off R (signed *Upper Booth*), all very pleasant tarmac work, leading to the farm at Upper Booth » SA through farm buildings, through gates and along good track (Pennine Way) towards steep climb of Jacob's Ladder » Debatable whether this is rideable, but it certainly is a massive challenge

2 From the top of the Ladder proceed SA passing Edale Cross » Continue through gates to the start of superb long descent, rocky at first, then easing before gate » SA down field to gate » SA, descending on good gravel track » Through gate, SA to join tarmac » SA descending steep hill » At base of hill take L fork (bridleway) uphill on tarmac road for 200m to sharp L cut back on rough path » Hard ascent bearing R towards summit, through gates eventually dropping down to join good hard pack track » Turn R then immediately L to descend to main road

3 L on road to first R on minor road then SA through gate to climb up tarmac road » SA on tarmac bridleway towards Hills Farm » Through farm, pushing bike, bear R through gate, then good climb up narrow track to summit plateau of Chinley Churn » Across moorland to gate and junction with bridleway, bear L (SA) on good rutted walled track » After 0.75km take bridleway R to descend fast and furiously, through gates to walled track, following stream to junction at head of Laneside Road

4 Fast tarmac descent of Laneside Road to junction with main New Mills to Hayfield road (A6015) » Turn L on road to lights » R up Union Road, L at mini roundabout, then L to **New Mills Central Station**

HOPE TO SHEFFIELD

GRADE: ▲

DISTANCE: 27KM TO WYMING BROOK + ADDITIONAL KM FOR RETURN INTO SHEFFIELD

TOTAL ASCENT: 928M

START: HOPE RAILWAY STATION

GRID REFERENCE: 181 832

FINISH: SHEFFIELD

CAFÉ: WOODBINE CAFÉ, HOPE Tel: 01433 621 407

PUBLIC HOUSE: APPARENTLY SHEFFIELD HAS A FEW TO CHOOSE FROM (So our testers told us)

NICKY BIRKIN ROUTE TESTING **PHOTO:** *ANDY HEADING*

Hope to Sheffield – East Peak

Introduction

One of the great things about living in, or close to, the city of Sheffield is the treasure trove of mountain biking delights that sits right on your doorstep.

To take advantage of this, and to give the environment a bit of a rest, here's a route for a car-free day: take a train then ride back to Steel City – of course, you can also get dropped off, but is this really in the spirit of things?

We've kept the riding fairly mellow throughout – covering the mileage is demanding enough, and there's a real killer of a climb near the end.

It is possible to extend this route into a real epic by exploiting any number of possibilities for link ups:

- Link up with the **Bradwell Circuit** *(see page 40)* into Castleton, then follow the **Mam Tor Classic** *(see page 122)* over Jaggers Clough to join at **Point 2** – tough!

- Start from Edale Station – follow the **Mam Tor Classic** *(see page 122)* again over Jaggers Clough to join at **Point 2**

- If you're still fired up with energy, link in the **Stanage Circuit** *(see page 130)* then join up with **Sheffield City Link 2 – Return** *(see page 184)*

The Ride

Starting from Hope Railway station, the route makes use of quiet back roads and then a tough, rocky bridleway to climb up and out onto Win Hill. Quality singletrack in a good situation carries you along this classic ridge, eventually joining a rocky and challenging descent to the Snake Pass (A57). From here it's a straightforward slog up to gain the height required for the classic Hagg Farm descent – a real snorter that leads to a satisfying cruise along the banks of Ladybower. Crossing the dam, the emphasis very much turns to 'up' as the route grinds along below Bamford Edge – the toil is well compensated for by some great views of the Hope Valley laid out below. This road then dips, allowing a brief respite before cutting out sharply towards Stanage Edge across some exposed and spectacular moorland – a very technical climb that few will cruise, especially at this stage! The descent from Stanage Pole is short but exhilarating – think quick and choose the best line.

Finally, quiet back roads lead to a couple of tasty downhill options to finish – depending on where you need to get back to in the city.

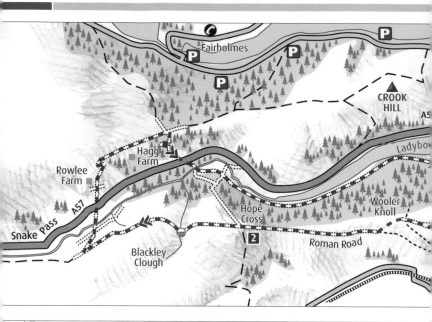

Fairholmes

CROOK
HILL

A5

Ladybo

Hagg
Farm

Rowlee
Farm

A57

Hope
Cross

Wooler
Knoll

Snake Pass

Blackley
Clough

2

Roman Road

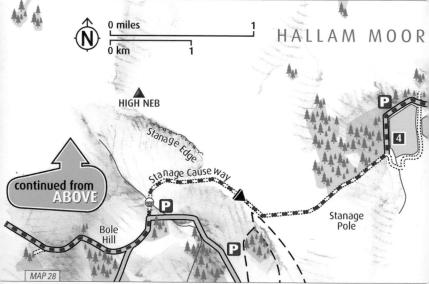

N

0 miles   1

0 km   1

HALLAM MOOR

HIGH NEB

Stanage Edge

Stanage Causeway

continued from
ABOVE

P

4

Bole
Hill

P

Stanage
Pole

P

MAP 28

Bamford

A6013

HATHERSAGE

WIN HILL

Shatton

Edge Farm

Aston

A6187

HOPE
STATION

0 miles   1

0 km   1

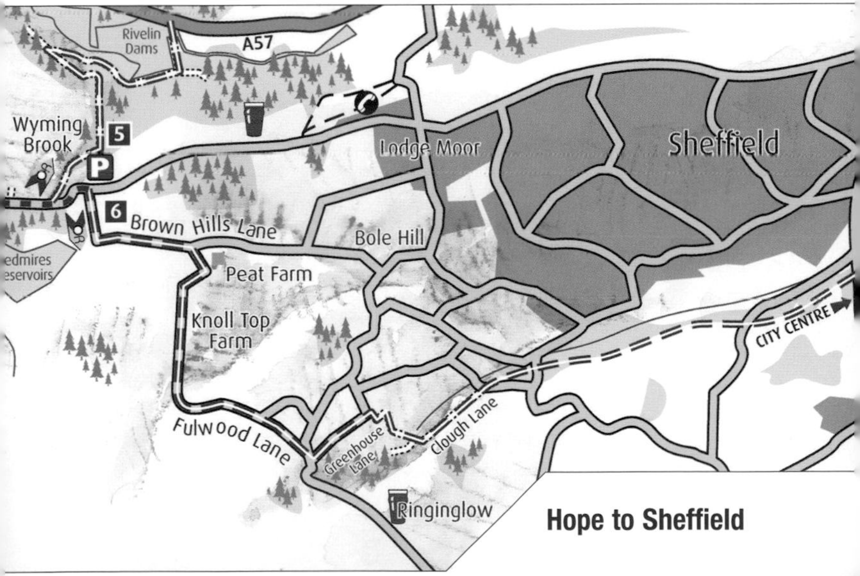

N

Rivelin
Dams

A57

Wyming
Brook   5

P

6   Brown Hills Lane

Lodge Moor

Sheffield

Bole Hill

edmires
reservoirs

Peat Farm

Knoll Top
Farm

CITY CENTRE

Fulwood Lane

Greenhouse
Lane

Clough Lane

Ringinglow

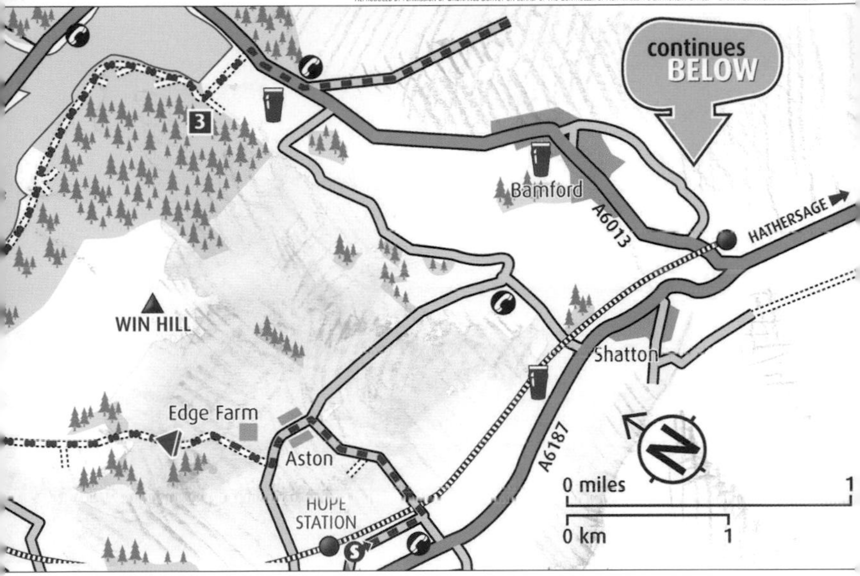

Hope to Sheffield

Directions – Hope to Sheffield

1 Turn L out of railway station, follow minor road, through gate, past factory to T-junction – turn L » Cross railway bridge, continue SA uphill, Parsons Lane, to T-junction at Aston » L through village, after road dips look out for sharp R turn uphill on tarmac (signposted *Win Hill and Hope Cross*) » L at Edge Farm » Uphill to join muddy walled bridleway » Climb track eventually levelling off slightly, undulating beneath the SW flank of Win Hill » At ridge, summit and junction with wide bridleway, descend L to join sandy track (Roman road), follow this to gate » Through gate then short climb to second gate at Hope Cross

2 SA up stony track, SA to gate » SA, cross stream at Blackley Clough, through awkward gate – after slight rise track descends » Great descent, very loose and stony to join tarmac » R through gate, steep descent on tarmac to cross stream, then up steeply to Snake Pass (A57) » **Cross busy and dangerous A57 with care**, SA up farm track » Continue through gate past Rowlee Farm, zig-zag up steep tarmac/gravel road which flattens off before reaching gate » SA through gate, continue up to second gate, through this to meet cross roads » Drop R, through gate into superb descent with bermed corners » Through gate, superb descent continues with loose and rocky sections, soon join hard pack, drop steeply and with care to A57 » Cross (still) busy and dangerous A57 with care » Through gate, down steep and often slippery descent » Curve R, cross bridge, continue L and then up track – often very muddy » Track forks at gate, L through gate and descend to S bank of Ladybower Reservoir » Easily R along track for 5km, finishing with easy climb up hard pack before track curves R and then descends to dam » Cross dam (note sign asking cyclists to dismount), join road, turn R

3 After approx. 0.5km, turn L opposite telephone box up steep tarmac hill » Continue SA below crags, ignore track on R » Road steepens, drops slightly then steepens again before dropping to junction with road coming up from R – turn L » Road curves L slightly to meet rough track coming down from crags at right angled corner, just after cattle grid – continue SA up this track, which soon curves round R becoming a loose, rocky and technical climb » As track emerges through gap in crags it levels out, bear L along double track towards Stanage Pole – good view point » Follow rough track down and L of pole and through gate to make short fast descent to join tarmac at Redmires Reservoir

4 Follow road LW, keeping reservoir on R, soon descending into hollow with car park on L

Two options here for your return to Sheffield:

for Hillsborough, Stannington, Crookes, Walkley, Broomhill etc:

5 **Wyming Brook**: Drop L into car park, pass through motorcycle barrier into woods and follow fast, rough track down to acute junction **»** Turn R at junction, SA along track through motorcycle barrier to join tarmac road leading L along dam wall, junction with A57 **»** Turn R with care onto busy A57, continue to where road splits: **»** Take R – A57 for *Crookes, Walkley, Broomhill* etc **»** Take L – A6101 for *Hillsborough, Stannington* etc. Keep your eyes open for bridleway options along this road.

for Fulwood, Ranmoor, Hunters Bar, Nether Edge etc:

6 Continue slightly uphill past car park on L to road junction, turn R onto Brown Hills Lane **»** Follow Brown Hills Lane as it bends L – SA to junction with Fulwood Lane – a steep hill **»** Turn R steeply up Fulwood Lane, follow this SA, passing a farm and then two turnings on L, look out for Greenhouse Lane – junction with **Sheffield City Link 1 – Out** *(see page 180)* either: **»** Link up with **Stanage Circuit** *(see page 130)* and return to Sheffield via Houndkirk Road and Blacka Moor – a good way to get over to Totley and Abbeydale, but a long day out **»** Return to Sheffield via *Porter Clough*: Turn L down Greenhouse Lane, descend for 500m on tarmac to join rough track, Clough Lane, dropping down R **»** Continue SA, fast descent to road **»** Continue SA across road, through gate, then follow walled track which eventually drops slightly to meet road **»** Continue SA across road, follow fun, undulating, waymarked bridleway through trees along L bank of stream **»** Continue SA, track emerges from trees and eventually meets another road at mini roundabout – cross over to park entrance and then follow your nose through Endcliffe Park to Hunters Bar Roundabout

Sheffield City Links

sponsored by **Singletrack**
mountain bike magazine

www.singletrackworld.co.uk

SECTION 6

Sheffield City Links

Sheffield City Link 1 – Out

Introduction

A useful way to extend the Stanage ride out from the city. The ride proper starts from the traditional meeting place at the entrance to Endcliffe Park, next to Hunters Bar roundabout. The way back in is described in **Sheffield City Link 2 – Return** *(see page 184)*.

The Ride

A pleasant cruise of around 5.5km takes you through leafy parkland to a hefty uphill as you ascend the loose track up Porter Clough. This eases soon enough to join tarmac and Fulwood Lane where you have the option of joining our **Stanage Circuit** *(see page 130)*. Congratulations – you are now in the Peak District.

Important Note: *Bridleways and footpaths often run parallel throughout these woods. Please try to keep to the bridleways only.*

SHEFFIELD CITY LINK 1 - OUT   GRADE: ▲

DISTANCE: 5.5KM
START: ENDCLIFFE PARK - HUNTERS BAR ENTRANCE
GRID REFERENCE: 333 858

TOTAL ASCENT: 264M
FINISH: FULWOOD LANE
CAFÉ: CAFÉS IN ENDCLIFFE PARK Tel: 0114 221 1900
AND AT FORGE DAM Tel: 0114 263 0751

PUBLIC HOUSE: THE NORFOLK ARMS, RINGINGLOW Tel: 0114 230 2197

Directions – Sheffield City Link 1 – Out

1 From the **Hunters Bar entrance to Endcliffe Park**, follow the path RW over little bridge crossing stream **»** Bear L, continue SA past fishing lake on R **»** Continue with stream on L, through trees to meet footbridge crossing stream on L **»** L over bridge, up to gate, through gate to meet Rustlings Road **»** Cross road by mini-roundabout, through park entrance on L – continue SA along marked cycle path

2 Continue past The Shepherd Wheel on R to meet Hangingwater Road, cross road, continue SA along bridleway to meet Whiteley Wood Road **»** Cross road, splash through ford then SA **»** On joining road turn L – look out for bridleway sign leading to gate, through gate then up brick track **»** SA along undulating track to meet road at gate, through gate, cross Woodcliffe Cottage Lane **»** SA along track, bear L then up slightly, eventually descending a little to commence stiff climb up **Porter Clough** on loose track **»** Track eases, eventually joining tarmac coming down from L **»** Up SA to join Fulwood Lane and **Stanage Circuit** at **Point 3**

PHOTO: *ANDY HEADING*

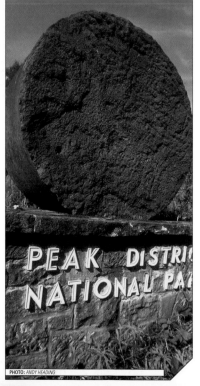

PHOTO: *ANDY HEADING*

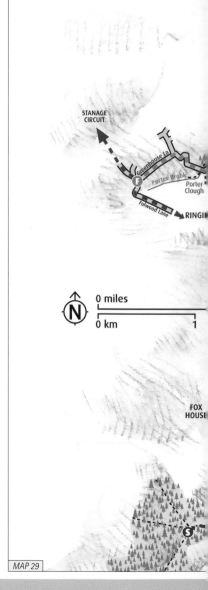

MAP 29

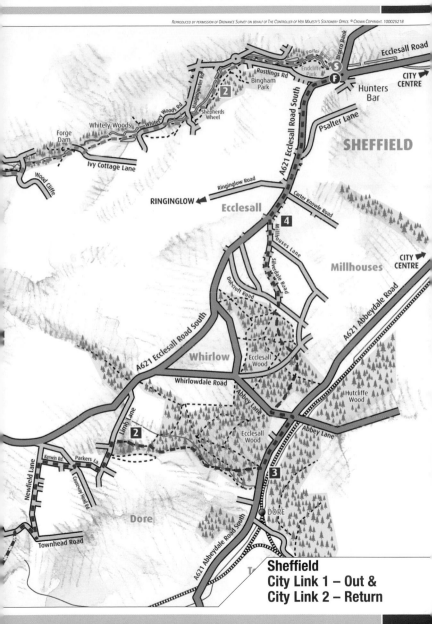

Sheffield
City Link 1 – Out &
City Link 2 – Return

Sheffield City Link 2 – Return

Introduction

The way back in for those who used the **Sheffield City Link 1 – Out** to get out *(see page 180).* **Negotiating** the maze of back streets through Dore, without getting lost, is now a very real possibility, even for newcomers.

The Ride

Great riding through very pleasant woodland, particularly in the spring when the bluebells are out.

SHEFFIELD CITY LINK 1 – RETURN   GRADE: ▲

DISTANCE: 8.4KM TO HUNTERS BAR   **TOTAL ASCENT:** 141M
START: SHORTS LANE, DORE   **FINISH:** HUNTERS BAR
GRID REFERENCE: 298 811
CAFÉ: WOODIES (HUNTERS BAR) Tel: 01142 676 122 **PUBLIC HOUSE:** PLENTY IN SHEFFIELD!

Directions – Sheffield City Link 2 – Return

1 Turn R at end of Shorts Lane (**Point 2b** on **Blacka Moor** or **Point 2** on **Stanage**) to join Whitelow Lane **»** Follow Whitelow Lane as it drops down steeply and then up **»** Turn acute L into Newfield Lane **»** Take 4th R into Kerwin Road, turn L at end and then almost immediately R into Parkers Lane **»** Turn L at end of Parkers Lane, by sports ground into Limb Lane **»** Roll down hill – look out for bridleway signposted on R just past dip in road (signposted *Abbeydale Road*)

2 Turn down this track – SA through gate **»** SA over bridge – at next gate turn L over bridge and immediately R **»** Follow track looking for blue bridleway arrows that indicate track to Abbeydale Road

3 Along Abbeydale Road to cross roads – turn L **»** Short climb to bridleway on R (just past Abbey Croft) **»** Follow bridleway SA, cross Whirlowdale Road, follow bridleway signs SA **»** Continue over 2 bridges – turn R between houses after 20m and out onto Dobcroft Road **»** SA up Silverdale Road then Millhouses Road leading to Ecclesall Road

4 Join the busy Ecclesall Road (A625) and head R – this leads directly back into the town centre via Hunters Bar roundabout

Appendixes

Tourist Information Offices

Glossop	Tel: 01457 855 920
Edale	Tel: 01433 670 207
Castleton National Park Information Centre	
	Tel: 01433 620 679
Buxton	Tel: 01298 25106

Weather

www.bbc.co.uk/weather   www.metoffice.com

Accommodation

Youth Hostels

YHA Buxton	Tel: 0870 770 5738
YHA Hathersage	Tel: 0870 770 5852
YHA Edale	Tel: 0870 770 5808
YHA Castleton	Tel: 0870 770 5758

Hotels, Self Catering & B&B

It's beyond the remit of this guide to give a full listing of tourist accommodation in The Peak. Here are a few places that have been recommended to us – but, being local, we've had no direct experience of these places ourselves.

Little John Hotel, Hathersage Tel: 01433 650 225
Roundmeadow Barn, Hope Tel: 01433 621 347
Blacksmiths Cottage, Hope (Next door to Woodbine Café)
Woodroffe Arms, Hope   Tel: 01433 620 531
Woodbine Café, Hope   Tel: 01433 621 407
Cheshire Cheese, Hope   Tel: 01433 620 330
Navigation Inn, Buxworth Tel: 01663 732 072
Waltzing Weasel, Birch Vale Tel: 01663 743 402

Camp Sites

Here are a couple that we can recommend for the summer months.

North Lees, Hathersage   Tel: 01433 650 838
Handy for the start of our Stanage Circuit.

Hardhurst Farm, near Hope   Tel: 01433 620 001
Has a café, close to the pub, handy for our Hope Valley rides.

Food and Drink

Cafés

The Peak District is fully geared up for mid-ride and post-ride refuelling sessions. Cafés vary from the distinctly 'twee' to the greasiest spoon – here's a good selection, mainly from the middle ground, all tried and tested by the team:

Woodbine Café, Hope   Tel: 01433 621 407
Log fire, very warm welcome, even for the muddiest, nice coffee and large portions of tasty home made pie and cake. Also does B&B.

Edale Cottage Café   Tel: 01433 670 293
Basic but good value café serving greasy spoon fare to all manner of enthusiasts from muddy, motorised and none motorised two wheeled transport. Variable opening times - e.g. 9-5 Sat & Sun in the winter.

Outside Café, Hathersage   Tel: **01433 651 936**
Upstairs above Outside in Hathersage - ideal for
the start/finish of our Hathersage route. A firm
favourite of climbers, walkers and roady cyclists.
Good selection of cakes and snacks.

Cottage Café, Castleton   Tel: **01433 670 293**
Variable opening times. Try not to muddy the
doilies.

Bank View Café, Langsett   Tel: **01226 762 337**
Can prove elusive! Roughly opposite the Wagon
and Horses inn – variable opening times.

Pubs

There are lots of good pubs in the Peak District –
all well worthy of a visit for post or mid-ride
refreshment. Here's a selection that can be
accessed from the routes in this guide.

The Norfolk Arms, Ringinglow
Good pub with a good beer garden. Unpretentious
and easily reached with just a small diversion
from our Stanage circuit.   Tel: **01142 302 197**

The Fox House
Recently tarted up into a modern gastro-pub,
The Fox house is a great place to sit outside and
enjoy a meal in the summer (just a pity the road
is so close). Very handy for the start/finish of our
Blacka Moor circuit.   Tel: **01433 631 708**

Ladybower Inn   Tel: **01433 651 241**
Next to a busy road, a bit bright inside, but the
best bet for our Ladybower based routes

Cheshire Cheese, Hope   Tel: **01433 620 330**
Small and full of character. Decent food, log fire,
also does B&B.

Travellers Rest, Hope   Tel: **01433 620 363**
Popular with climbers as well as cyclists.
Offers excellent bar meals, and a good pint of
Barnsley bitter.

Pubs in Castleton – take your pick, plenty to
choose from in the Hope Valley's premier tourist
honey pot.

Waltzing Weasel, Birch Vale Tel: **01663 743 402**
Brilliant bar meals – the best we've tasted.

The Royal Hotel, Hayfield Tel: **01633 742 721**
Good pub – often busy.

Cat and Fiddle   Tel: **01298 23364**
Welcoming pub in an exposed and atmospheric
location. Visit the biker's bar for a mid-route stop
on our Buxton circuit, then summon up your
courage and bravely cross the A537.

Bike Shops

High Peak Cycles, 93 High Street West, Glossop
Tel: 01457 861 535

KG Bikes, 13 Norfolk Street, Glossop
Tel: 01457 862 427

Sett Valley Cycles, 9 Union Road, New Mills
Tel: 01633 742 629

The Bike Factory, Beech Road, Whaley Bridge
Tel: 01663 735 020

JE James, 347-361 Bramall Lane, Sheffield
Tel: 0114 255 0557
&
Progress House, Brimington Road North,
Chesterfield. Tel: 01246 453 453

Langsett Cycles, 182-192 Infirmary Road,
Sheffield
Tel: 0114 234 8191

Bike Hire

Forgotten to bring your bike?
Derwent Cycle Hire, Fairholmes, Ladybower
Tel: 01433 651 261

Outdoor Shops

Not bike shops, but useful for maps, clothing,
energy bars etc.
Outside, Hathersage & Calver
Nevisport, Hathersage
CCC, Hathersage
Hitch 'n' Hike, Hope 'n' Bamford
The Outdoor Shop, Castleton

Other Publications

Mountain Bike Guide: *Quality Routes in the*
Peak District and Derbyshire
Mike Pearce, Ernest Press

Mountain Bike Guide:
Derbyshire and the Peak District
Tim Banton, Andy Spencer, Tom Windsor,
Ernest Press

Mountain Biking in The Peak District
Paul Wake and Paul Woodrow, Sigma Leisure

Off-Beat Cycling and Mountain Biking in
the Peak District
Clive Smith, Sigma Leisure

About the Authors

Paul Evans
Creative Director of Vertebrate Graphics,
Paul has been mountain biking for two full
decades, mainly in the Peak District. When not
riding his local trails, Paul enjoys mountainous
excursions in the Lakes and North Wales
(i.e. he doesn't mind carrying his bike!) - and he's
no stranger to enduro events, having recently
made a respectable time at the Dyfi event near
Machynnlleth. Paul also enjoys time with his
family, snowboarding, surfing and climbing.

Jon Barton
Living in the heart of the Hope Valley, Jon is
an authority on all things to do with the Peak.
Having climbed and cycled in the area for
decades, Jon can be relied upon for expert advice
on all manner of mtb routes. Doesn't like
descending, finds singletrack too awkward, and
usually carries uphill.

About the photographers

John Houlihan, at Witness photography

John is a seven time Polaris winner, was the highest placed Britain with 9th place in the World Mountain Bike Orienteering Championships (MTBO) 2002 and is the 2004 British MTBO champion. A full time photojournalist his work is regularly commissioned by the Sunday Times, The Guardian, What Mountain Bike among many. He is currently chairman of the Trail Cyclist Association, the national governing body for mountain bike orienteering in the UK and is one of only two Britains fully qualified as International MTBO controllers for world cup and world championship events.

He is currently devoting more time to Adventure Racing, between his family commitments and rebuilding his house.

Andy Heading

At the end of each Peak District ride, Andy regrets living at the top of a big, steep hill on the outskirts of Matlock. A professional sports photographer, his 20 years as a mountain biker have included trips to Ethiopia, Romania, Morocco and China, and racing wins in Polaris, Trailquest and the 1,097-mile **Iditasport Impossible** across Alaska.

Vertebrate Graphics

Vertebrate Graphics is Britain's leading graphic design agency that specialises in the outdoor leisure market.

Vertebrate Graphics has had substantial success in the design and production of specialist outdoor books. These include Hillwalking – The Official Handbook of the Mountain Leader and Walking Group Leader schemes (a best-selling outdoor title for two years running), and two highly praised guidebooks for rock climbers - Selected Rock Climbs in The Lake District and Staffordshire Gritstone.

> **This is the first of our series of mountain biking guides – look out for further titles covering The Yorkshire Dales, Wales and The South West, which will be on the shelves soon.**
>
> www.**v-graphics**.co.uk